⋙ CONTENTS ⋘

≫ WELCOME ≪

MY FIRST VISIT TO DETROIT was last January. A cruel time of year, for sure. There's a dry, frozen-river cold that sinks into your bones. You imagine those first auto factories and you just shiver. Luckily, the city is gifted with wonderful corner bars like Abick's and The Bronx, and for those first few trips they warmed me up. Before January, my Detroit was a mixture of Pistons basketball, Elmore Leonard, a dozen Motown choruses and, of late, the shock-value headlines that we'd all read. Detroit Calls It Quits. The Motor City Goes Bust. Detroit Rock Bottom.

I chose to explore Detroit in the bleak of winter. Let's do the thing, I thought. Let's see the city in the mean cold light. The heavy burden of race. The emptying urban core. The woes of violent crime. As local columnist, John Carlisle, would tell me later, "We can't hide from ourselves here." Detroit is an honest city, maybe the most honest in the world — which is one reason we love it. Its authenticity is everywhere.

The rock bottom is apparent, sure. The abandoned buildings and crippling poverty. But I see more, too. I see a well of good ideas. Urban farmers transforming lots of blight into acres of bounty. A small business hub in Corktown, with coffee roasters and metalsmiths and ladies sewing winter coats that double as sleeping bags. And I see soul. Folks who've endured the last forty years. Small business owners like Lonzo Jackson, city employees like Maggie Townsend, a revival of young black entrepreneurs. All over town, I encounter small victories, an arsenal of ingenuity that is encouraging, but also begs the question: Will this ingenuity serve the majority who struggle on the margins?

Things in Detroit are complicated. They are both better and worse than you'd think. Everyday is both winter and summer. This book is about both, about the whole of Detroit. Old and new, broken and beautiful.

My last trip into town in May, I was driving down Mack Avenue and a pheasant nearly flew into my windshield. The bird was a three-foot flash of golden-brown, something you'd never expect a mile from skyscrapers. The moment spoke of Detroit in restoration mode. A reboot, even if wild. Where the city will find itself in ten or twenty or fifty years, who knows? For me, I cling to the words of a poet, Detroit's own Naomi Long Madgett, who mediates on the future with this line: "The grandchildren are upstairs dreaming." *-TB*

ESSENTIALS

TRANSPORT

TAXI
Uber
uber.com

....

PRIVATE CAR
Luxury Limousine
313-582-8970
luxurylimousinedearborn.com

....

BICYCLE RENTAL
Wheelhouse
1340 E Atwater Street
wheelhousedetroit.com

HOTELS

DOWNTOWN
Westin Book Cadillac
1114 Washington Blvd
bookcadillacwestin.com

....

BOUTIQUE
Inn at Ferry Street
84 E. Ferry Ave
innonferrystreet.com

....

DESIGN
Honor and Folly
Michigan Ave
honorandfolly.com

BUSINESS

MORNING MEETING
Rowland Café
Guardian Building
therowlandcafe.com

CLIENT DINNER
Selden Standard
3921 2nd Ave
seldenstandard.com

....

NIGHTCAP
Cliff Bell's
2030 Park Ave
cliffbells.com

CALENDAR

JAN   International Auto Show
FEB   Tattoo Expo
MAR   Marche du Nain Rouge
APR   MLB Opening Day
MAY   Movement Festival
JUN   Detroit Grand Prix
JUL   Gold Cup
AUG   Jazz Festival
SEP   Dally in the Alley
OCT   Fall Beer Festival
NOV   Campus Martius Tree
DEC   Noel Night

BOOKS

☞ *Engines of Change*
   by Paul Ingrassia
☞ *Detroit City Is the Place to Be*
   by Mark Binelli
☞ *Middlesex*
   by Jeffrey Eugenides

BLOGS

crainsdetroit.com
deadlinedetroit.com
sweet-juniper.com

ONE DAY

Rivera murals at DIA

Slows Barbecue

Cliff Bell's jazz

....

WEEKEND

Astro coffee

Eastern Market

Motown Museum

Pure Detroit's Guardian Tour

Midtown shops, Shinola and Nora

Baker's Keyboard Lounge

FOODWAY

Coneys

Natural-cased beef dogs slathered with spiced-up, beanless chili, topped with mustard and onions, and chomped on the go.

RECORD COLLECTION

The Supremes ....*Where Did Our Love Go*

Derrick May...*Rhythim is Rhythim*

Bob Seger and the Silver Bullet Band ....*Night Moves*

White Stripes...*Elephant*

Marvin Gaye .... *What's Going On*

Funkadelic...*Maggot Brai*

McKinney's Cotton Pickers ....*Crying and Sighing*

Slum Village ....*Fan-Tas-Tic, Vol.* 1

Aretha Franklin............................*I Never Loved a Man the Way I Love You*

Stevie Wonder ....*Songs in the Key of Life*

John Lee Hooker...*The Blues*

The Stooges ....*The Stooges*

Eminem.. *The Marshall Mathers LP*

Jackie Wilson ....*Mr. Excitement!*

MC5..*Kick Out the Jams*

Yusef Lateef ....*Psychicemotus*

ESSENTIALS

PROGRESS

↳ Hotel stays up 68% in 2012
↳ Named one of seven Google Tech Hub Hotspots in 2013
↳ Quicken buys 2 million square feet of downtown office space
↳ Whole Foods opens 21,000 square foot space in Midtown
↳ More than 100,000 techno fans attend Movement Festival in 2013
↳ Afterhouse Detroit transforms abandoned homes into greenhouses
↳ Nine philanthropies pledge $330 million to save city art collection

PROBLEMS

↳ Only 3% of third graders test on-grade level in math in 2011
↳ Fifth least fit city in America
↳ Over 70% of city work force does not reside in Detroit
↳ Roughly 78,000 structures in the city sit vacant
↳ Murder cases down 14% since 2012, still highest rate among big cities
↳ Downtown Detroit's residential occupancy is at 99%, waiting lists at nearly every building
↳ Burglary offenses down 19% in 2013 from previous year
↳ Fastest growing number of carless households in America

SOCIAL GOOD

Hatch Detroit, The Empowerment Plan, Write A House, D-YES, Detroit SOUP, Detroit Beautification Project, Mt. Elliott Makerspace, The Blight Authority, Arise Detroit, Hostel Detroit, D:Hive, Detroit Food Academy, Youth Transit Alliance, Avalon Breads, Detroit Venture Partners

STATISTICS

$18.5 billion ....Largest municipal bankruptcy case in U.S. history, 2013
1.86 million..Peak population of the city, 1950
1,500.............................Empty lots to form world's largest urban tree farm
400 ....Teach for America volunteers in Detroit
$37,000 ....Median home sales price in city of Detroit in 2013

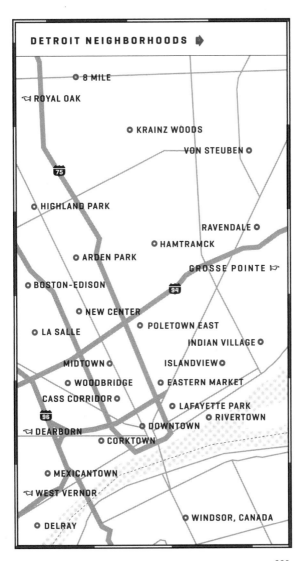

DETROIT NEIGHBORHOODS ➡

- 8 MILE
- ROYAL OAK
- KRAINZ WOODS
- VON STEUBEN
- 75
- HIGHLAND PARK
- RAVENDALE
- HAMTRAMCK
- ARDEN PARK
- GROSSE POINTE
- BOSTON-EDISON
- 94
- NEW CENTER
- POLETOWN EAST
- LA SALLE
- INDIAN VILLAGE
- MIDTOWN
- ISLANDVIEW
- WOODBRIDGE
- EASTERN MARKET
- CASS CORRIDOR
- LAFAYETTE PARK
- 96
- RIVERTOWN
- DEARBORN
- DOWNTOWN
- CORKTOWN
- MEXICANTOWN
- WEST VERNOR
- WINDSOR, CANADA
- DELRAY

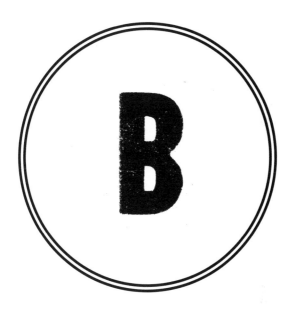

BESTS

*A curated list of citywide favorites including coffee shops,
donut dives, pizzerias, live jazz, yacht clubs, hat makers,
vinyl collectors, printmakers and more*

⫸ FOOD & DRINK ⫷

DONUTS
Dutch Girl
19000 Woodward Ave
Palmer Park
313-368-3020
Homemade blueberry cake, bulletproof glass window.
....

COFFEESHOP
Astro
2124 Michigan Ave
Corktown
astrodetroit.com
Trendy espresso pulls, a smart staff and a quippy chalkboard menu.
....

BAGELS
Institute of Bagels
1236 Michigan Ave
Corktown
Boiled-and-baked by Ben Newman, served plain or as healing sandwiches.

GREASY SPOON
The Clique
1326 E. Jefferson Ave
Rivertown
313-259-0922
Greasy diner where local movers and shakers hob nob over hashbrowns.
....

BBQ
Slows
2138 Michigan Ave
Corktown
slowsbarbq.com
Buzzy pork and cornbread from the Cooley family.
....

CONEYS
Lafayette
118 W Lafayette
Downtown
Nothing says latenight like messy hot dogs from a centuryold downtown dive.

AMERICAN
Craft Work
8047 Agnes St
West Village
craftworkdetroit.com
American favorites like whole trout. Wonderful bar side.
....

CUBAN
Vicente's
1250 Library St
Downtown
vicente.us
Havana in Michigan: cinnamon sangria, Ropa Vieja and salsa dancing.
....

DINER
Rose's Fine Food
10551 E Jefferson
Belle Isle
734-330-3241
Brand new with a brunch line worth the wait.

PIZZA

Supino
1457 Russell St
Eastern Market
supinopizzeria.com
Redefining 'Detroit-style,' if you can get a seat: thin-crust pies and six tables.

....

SLIDERS

Green Dot
2200 W Lafayette Blvd
Corktown
greendotstables.com
This is the UN of sliders: the Cuban, Korean, and Mystery Meat all $3.

....

TACOS

Taqueria Lupita's
3443 Bagley St
Mexicantown
313-843-1105
Hole-in-the-wall with authentic al pastor and freshly-made salsas.

....

CAJUN

Louisiana Creole
Gumbo
2051 Gratiot Ave
Eastern Market
detroitgumbo.com
Spicy red beans and rice, shrimp gumbo to-go.

TAPAS

La Feria
4130 Cass Ave
Downtown
laferiadetroit.com
Channeling spring in Seville with small plates like herby sardines on toast.

....

MEXICAN-ITALIAN

El Barzon
3710 Junction St
Mexicantown
313-894-2070
Barbacoa and bolognaise under the same roof: normal, no. Delicious, yes.

....

POLISH

Polish Village Café
2990 Yemans St
Hamtramck
polishvillagecafe.us
Golden child of Hamtramck: pierogi and dill pickle soup from a hotel basement.

....

FISH & CHIPS

Scotty Simpson's
22200 Fenkell
Brightmoor
scottysfishandchips.com
A family affair of golden-battered fried-to-order fish since 1950.

STEAK

Roast
1128 Washington Blvd
Downtown
roastdetroit.com
Michael Symon's upscale ode-to-carnivores in the Book Cadillac.

....

SPORTS BAR

Nemo's
1384 Michigan Ave
Corktown
nemosdetroit.com
One-stop-shop for day-drinking, game-day stadium shuttle.

....

COCKTAILS

Sugar House
2130 Michigan Ave.
Corktown
sugarhousedetroit.com
Sophisticated speakeasy and a 21-page, mixologist's dream menu.

....

JAZZ BAR

Baker's Keyboard
Lounge
20510 Livernois Ave
Eight Mile-Livernois
313-345-6300
A Coltrane-vibe and a piano-shaped bar at world's oldest jazz club.

»» SHOPPING ««

PAPER GOODS
City Bird
460 W. Canfield St.
Midtown
ilovecitybird.com
For the Midwestern gift-giver, elevated tchotchkes and a wall of cards.

....

HARDWARE
Busy Bee
1401 Gratiot Ave.
Eastern Market
A mom-and-pop hardware mainstay that'll make you want to fix stuff.

....

MEN'S STYLE
Hugh
4240 Cass Ave.
Midtown
lovehughlongtime.com
From highball glasses to shaving brushes.

INSTRUMENTS
Custom Music International
1930 Hilton Rd
Ferndale
customtubas.com
The shiniest of tubas, flutes and bassoons.

....

WATCHES
Shinola
441 W. Canfield St.
Midtown
shinola.com
WWII-era brand re-launched as American-made timepieces.

....

BOOKS
John K. King Used and Rare Books
901 W. Lafayette
Downtown
Housed in a converted warehouse, book-lover's hideaway.

KEYS
Fred's Key Shop
3470 2nd Ave.
Midtown
fredskeyshop.com
Just three brothers picking Detroiters' locks since 1962.

....

BODEGA
Parker Street Market
1814 Parker St
West Village
parkerstreetmarket.com
Neighborhood store for local produce, food goods and fresh Drought juices.

....

HATS
Henry the Hatter
1307 Broadway
Downtown
Dobbs to Stetson, "Detroit's Exclusive Hatter" since 1893.

BICYCLES

The Hub

3611 Cass Ave.
Midtown
thehubofdetroit.org

Cheap tune-ups, smart fixer-uppers and the Back Alley youth bike program.

....

DENIM

Detroit Denim

detroitdenim.com

Channeling the past at Ponyride with meticulously-made jeans for today.

....

SKATEBOARDING

CHIIPSS

Hamtramck
10229 Joseph
Campau Ave.
chiipps.com

Skateboard-centered clothing, shoes, decks; make a trial run on the on-site ramp.

....

HOME

Nest

460 W Canfield St
Midtown
nestdetroit.com

General store feel, oak shelves full of handpicked housewares.

LOCAL GOODS

Detroit Mercantile Company

3434 Russell St.
Eastern Market
detroitmercantile.com

Americana-bent, Detroit-centric makers in former firehouse.

....

CANDY

Leddy's Wholesale Candy

15928 Grand
River Ave
Grandmont Rosedale

Glorious rows of rock candy, gumdrops and more.

....

RECORDS

Peoples Records

1464 Gratiot Ave
Midtown
peoplesdetroit.com

A crate-digger's heaven for soul and funk, manned by Brad Hales.

....

ART COLLECTIVE

Public Pool

3309 Caniff Ave
Hamtramck
apublicpool.com

Artspace and venue, part organization-part organism.

MEXICAN GROCERY

Honeybee Market

2443 Bagley Ave.
Mexicantown
honeybeemkt.com

Come to shop the meat counter, kickin' spice section and the best to-go guac.

....

AMERICANA

Willys

441 W. Canfield St
Midtown
willysdetroit.com

Distinct and beloved brands [Filson, Mollusk Surf] in former motor company digs.

....

SALVAGE

Architectural Salvage Warehouse

4885 15th St.
Corktown
aswdetroit.org

Enormous cavern of deconstructed local building materials, priced to go.

....

FLOWERS

Fresh Cut

W. Forest & Rosa Parks
freshcutdetroit.com

Sarah Pappas's 10-week bouquet service for $150.

≫ ACTION ≪

JAZZ

Cliff Bell's
2030 Park Avenue
Downtown
cliffbells.com
Doorman Rosie welcomes jazz hepcats to the Art Deco, circa-1935 hotspot.

....

FESTIVAL

Dally in the Alley
Cass Corridor
dallyinthealley.com
Festival since 1977 draws thousands every September.

....

COFFEE CLASS

Anthology
1401 Vermont St
Corktown
anthologycoffee.com
Fancy coffee drinkers get schooled [for free] by the Ponyride pros.

GARDENS

Belle Isle
Conservatory
876 Picnic Way
Belle Isle
Monticello-style glass dome with roses, orchids rescued during WWII.

....

RUSSIAN BATHS

The Schvitz
8295 Oakland St
North End
Former gangster's cave with 150-degree plaitza and naked devotees.

....

THEATER

Redford
17360 Lahser Rd
Old Redford
redfordtheatre.com
Classic 10-rank pipe organ, enough seats for 1,500.

DRIVE-IN

Ford Wyoming
10400 Ford Rd
Dearborn
forddrivein.com
Two movies, one ticket, at America's largest drive-in.

....

OKTOBERFEST

The Dakota Inn
Rathskeller
17324 John R St
Highland Park
dakota-inn.com
German beer den, where Gemutlichkeit flows, opened in 1933 by Kurz family.

....

SAILING

Detroit Yacht Club
Belle Isle
dyc.com
Founded in 1868, private boathouse along Nautical Mile.

HYDROPLANE

Detroit Gold Cup
Detroit River
gold-cup.com
Thunderously loud,
200-mph hydro-
races considered
Super Bowl of
power boating.

....

KARAOKE

Bert's Marketplace
1727 Russell Ave
Eastern Market
bertsentertainment-
complex.com
Soulful spot plugs
in Motown karaoke
mic every Saturday,
11am until 8pm.

....

FEATHERBOWLING

Cadieux Café
4300 Cadieux Rd
East Side
cadieuxcafe.com
Trappist ales,
steamed mussels
and the only place
in America for
Belgium-style bocce.

....

RACE

Thunderdrome
Mound Rd & Outer Dr
Eight Mile
thunderdrome.com
Woodstock on two
wheels, they say,
around resurrected
velodrome track.

....

URBAN TRAIL

Dequindre Cut
Rivertown
detroitriverfront.org
Once a rail line, this
sweet 1.3-miler for
bikes and foot traffic
runs to Eastern
Market.

....

ROLLER RINK

Northland
22311 W 8 Mile Rd
Far West Side
northlandrink.com
Sixty years strong
and a packed rink
most nights. Cou-
ples with smooth
skills welcomed.

....

RUIN

Packard Plant
East Grand Blvd
detroiturbex.com
Kahn-designed
decay that's spookily
beautiful, not safe
for trekking around.

....

PRINTMAKING

Salt & Cedar
1448 Riopelle St
Eastern Market
saltandcedar.com
Range of expert-led
workshops, from
'zines to papermak-
ing to letterpress
posters.

....

ROCKABILLY

Painted Lady
Lounge
1930 Jacob St
Hamtramck
313-874-2991
Pink-and-green
punk bar with
dancefloor, cheap
beer and live bands
every weekend.

....

BOWLING

Garden Bowl
4140 Woodward Ave
Midtown
majesticdetroit.com
Oldest in the US,
perfect for mid-
winter's night —
the glow pins!
— until 2am.

....

BIKERIDE

Slow Roll
Citywide
slowroll.bike
@detroitbikecity
Super-friendly
Monday night
group rides for all
ages and all paces.

⫸ EXPERTISE ⫷

SUSTAINABILITY
Green Garage
*4444 Second Ave
Midtown
greengaragedetroit.com*
Triple bottomline
incubator and model
for how to retrofit
green spaces.
....

FOOD EDUCATION
Detroit Food
Academy
*Citywide
detroitfoodacademy.com*
School-based food
education with social
enterprise vision.
....

TRAVEL BLOGGING
Meghan McEwan
designtripper.com
Super-stylish travel
picks, Michigan and
beyond, from the
delightful owner of
Honor & Folly.

METALSMITHING
Smith Shop
*1401 Vermont St
Corktown
smithshopdetroit.com*
Classes, workshops
and beautiful archi-
tectural hardware,
based in Ponyride
enclave.
....

URBAN FARM
Brother Nature
Check out Greg and
Olivia's Corktown
bounty at Eastern
Market, Shed #2,
on Saturdays,
and on Facebook.
....

VENTURE CAPITAL
Detroit Venture
Partners
*1555 Broadway
Downtown
detroitventurepart-
ners.com*
Smart thinkers, fast
movers with a focus
in early stage tech
start-ups.
....

BLIGHT
The Blight Authority
*719 Griswold
theblightauthority.com*
Clearing hundreds
of eyesores from city
neighborhoods, start-
ing with Brightmoor.
....

LETTERPRESS
Signal Return
*1345 Division St
Eastern Market
signalreturnpress.org*
Community shop
with mammoth
19th century presses
and a full workshop
calendar.
....

FILMMAKING
The Work

Rivertown
theworkinc.com
Video projects
with Chevy and
Lincoln, plus an epic
X Games Detroit
promo reel.

....

PIANO RESTORATION
Master Piano
495 West Forest Ave
mprpiano.com
Appraisals, pur-
chases, moves and
repairs that make
the sparkly whites
sing again.

....

BARBER
Social Club
Grooming
5272 Anthony Wayne Dr
Midtown
313-832-4950
Sebastian Jackson's
bringing an all-races
goodwill to the clas-
sic barber shop.

....

ACROBATICS
Detroit Flyhouse
3434 Russell St
Eastern Market
detroitflyhouse.com
Part yoga, part
Cirque du Soleil
using silks, hoops
and trapeze bars, a
serious workout.

RUNNING
RUNdetroit
441 W Canfield St
Midtown
run-detroit.com
Training regimes,
city routes and Sat-
urday morning runs
— rain or shine.

....

PICKLING
McClure's
8201 St. Aubin St
mcclurespickles.com
Grandma Lala's
secret brine led to
relishes, potato
chips, and a cult fol-
lowing of pickles.

....

CREATIVE STUDIO
Skidmore
1555 Broadway
Downtown
Skidmorestudio.com
First opened in
1959, relocated back
downtown in recent
years to Madison
Building.

....

DEVELOPMENT
The Cooley Family
Corktown
ponyride.org
Neighborhood 2.0
vision of collabora-
tion and generos-
ity, Slow's Bar-B-Q,

Sugar House,
Ponyride and more.

....

DOGS
Canine to 5
3443 Cass Ave
Midtown
Caninetofivedetroit.com
Best pup boarding
and grooming in
town, needed ven-
ture with the strays
epidemic.

....

COLUMNIST
John Carlisle
Detroit Free Press
freep.com
Soulful, award-
winning profiles
of forgotten locals
written with heart.

....

ARCHITECTURAL DESIGN
Kaija Woullet
laavudesign.com
Modern sensibility,
simple materials,
Slow's and the new
Gold Cash Gold.

....

BEARDS
Beard Balm
beardbalm.us
Food-grade oils,
good for your face
and [supposedly]
good for your
marriage.

ALMANAC

*A deep dive into the cultural heritage of Detroit through
timelines, how-to's, newspaper clippings, letters, lists,
rock reviews and other historical hearsay*

HISTORY OF MOTOWN RECORDS

After modest success as a songwriter, city native Berry Gordy launched his Detroit record company at the age of 29, spinning an $800 family loan into the most universally beloved catalogue of record gold in American history. In the 1960s, the label scored more than 100 top ten hits with hometown artists such as Little Stevie Wonder, The Supremes and Smokey Robinson. Today, the original "Hitsville, U.S.A." - one of eight Grand Boulevard houses that Motown would own - hosts 90-minute historical tours that include a quick dance lesson. motownmuseum.com

Berry Gordy returns from Korea, begins songwriting....................1953
Gordy starts first record label with $800 family loan....................1959
The Miracles release "Shop Around" on Motown........................1960
Gordy signs Steveland "Stevie Wonder" Morris, age 11 1961
The Primettes change name to The Supremes 1961
First Motor Town Revue tours American South 1962
"Heatwave" by Martha and the Vendellas.......................................1963
"The Way You Do the Things You Do" by The Temptations 1964
Mary Wells leaves Motown after Billboard #1, "My Guy" 1964
Temptations' "My Girl" hits #1 1965
"Stop in the name of Love" by The Supremes 1965
Gladys Knight and the Pips sign 1966
Name changes to Diana Ross and the Supremes 1967
Berry Gordy buys "Motown Mansion" in Detroit........................1967
Motown records hold top three spots on Billboard 1968
"I Heard It through the Grapevine" by Marvin Gaye 1968
The Jackson 5 audition for Berry Gordy.......................................1968
"Signed, Sealed, Delivered I'm Yours" by Stevie Wonder 1970
"I Want You Back" by The Jackson 5..1970
Smokey Robinson's first #1 hit, "Tears of a Clown"......................1970
Gordy and Diana Ross welcome a daughter...................................1971
Michael Jackson, age 13, on cover of *Rolling Stone*...................1971
Funk Brothers, famed session musicians, dismissed.....................1972
Motown moves headquarters to Hollywood 1972
Motown 25 television show celebrates label's birthday.................1983
Marvin Gaye shot and killed by his father in L.A. 1984

STREET CARS

The Critic
April 4, 1890

CROWDS who watched the progress of the new electric car in Detroit this week wondered that it went along so smoothly and so well. That electric cars have got to come to Detroit now goes without saying, but the people who wondered at the ten-mile-an-hour speed of the street car last Wednesday can but marvel at what has been accomplished by electricity in the matter of rapid transit. In the current number of Scribner's is an article by an eminent electrician, stating that on a circular trial track in the east an electric car, on which the wheels are propelled directly by the armature, is actually making the unheard of speed of 120 miles an hour, and making it without and special effort either...At this rate of speed, a man may reside in Detroit or Chicago as a suburb of New York and run down to the metropolis mornings to business, or he may run down to Cleveland or Cincinnati to save the bother of telegraphing. He wouldn't reach his destination quite as quick as though he were traveling in a canon ball, but he would come pretty near it. Jules Verne is already beginning to be looked upon as altogether too slow for a nineteenth century prophet.

OJIBWA

Present-day Detroit was the third main settlement locale for the Ojibwa tribe, after Montreal and Niagara Falls.

amik .... beaver
mooz .... moose
ajijaak .... sandhill crane
biigokokwe'owesi .... whip-poor-will
goon .... snow
giizis .... sun, moon
ogimaa .... chief
ogichidaa .... warrior
nimaamaa .... mother
gichi-mookomaan .... white person

JIMMY HOFFA'S DISAPPEARANCE

Labor union leader Jimmy Hoffa, who grew up in Detroit, was last seen outside the Machus Red Fox Restaurant, a suburban restaurant, at around 2:45 PM on July 30, 1975. Below are three theories explaining his disappearance.

BURIED IN MICHIGAN Several tips have led to the FBI digging up residential backyards. In 2004, authorities searched the home of Frank Sheeran, a former friend of Hoffa's, who claimed responsibility. They found blood, but not Hoffa's.

A BARREL IN FLORIDA In 1982, a mob hitman named Charles Allen testified to a U.S. Senate committee that Hoffa had been shot and that his body had been grounded up, put in a steel drum, shipped to Florida and dumped into a swamp.

GIANTS STADIUM IN NEW JERSEY In a 1989 interview with Playboy magazine, mob hit man Donald "Tony the Greek" Frankos said he had heard that two hit men from New Jersey has carried out the hit and subsequent burial of Hoffa's body in one of the end zones at Giants Stadium. The stadium was under construction when Hoffa went missing, but when the building was demolished in 2010 no evidence was found.

MOWER GANG

In 2010, mower-in-chief Tom Nardone and his band of volunteer grasshounds first took to the urban prairie. Riding and pushing their way across dozens of unkempt and forgotten parks and playgrounds, the crew has taken grassroots initiative to a new level. Today, the Mower Gang cares for more than 90 spaces, meeting every other Wednesday with grass cutters and weed whackers, and annually doing a 24-hour "Mow-town" marathon. This winter the do-gooders even began shoveling snow. Well done, mowers. *mowergang.com*

AUTOMOBILES OF NOTE

Make & Model	Description... Year
Curved Dash Oldsmobile	*Open, runabout-style seated two...1900*
Anderson Detroit Electric	*First battery-powered vehicle...1907*
Ford Model T	*Built cheap and fast at Piquette Plant, available in gray, blue, green and red. No black yet...1908*
Cadillac Model 30	*Enclosed body with electric starter...1912*
Packard's Twin Six	*Luxury Touring's popular abroad...1915*
Hupmobile	*Handsome pioneer of freewheeling...1928*
Cadillac V16	*High-powered, 6,600-pound dame was company's costliest car at the time...1930*
Chrysler Airflow	*Sleek body inspired by geese...1934*
Willys MB Jeep	*WWII Army vehicles of choice for cross-country recon missions...1941*
Cadillac Eldorado Biarritz	*Red bullet lights, sharp tail fins...1959*
Lincoln Continental	*Well-known suicide doors, first 2-year bumper-to-bumper warranty in US...1961*
Chevrolet Bel Air	*First car James Bond drove on film...1962*
Corvette Stingray	*Hidden flip lights, split rear view...1963*
Ford Mustang GT	*McQueen's Highland green fastback made famous in the film, Bullitt...1968*
Dodge Challenger	*Rival to Mustang and Camaro...1970*
Buick Riviera	*Arched fenders, muscly stance...1971*
GMC Suburban	*Four-door, rounded line, 19 years...1973*
Ford F-Series	*Best-selling US vehicle, 32 years...1982*
Chrysler Minivan	*Launched a thousand soccer moms...1984*
Jeep Grand Wagoneer	*Final year of beloved woody SUV...1991*

THE HEIDELBERG PROJECT

Artist Tyree Guyton's large-scale installation of reimagined abandoned homes, works of monumental whimsy that use vinyl records, pennies and stuffed animals, have survived bouts of arson and political bullying and continue to drawn global acclaim and adoration. Below, a selection of the Heidelberg structures and their fate. 3600 Heidelberg Street, heidelberg.org

Structure	Fate
"Baby Boy House"	*Demolished in 1991 by order of Mayor*
"Fun House"	*Demolished in 1991 by order of Mayor*
"Truck Stop"	*Demolished in 1991 by order of Mayor*
"Your World"	*Demolished in 1999 by order of Mayor*
"Happy Feet"	*Demolished in 1999 by order of Mayor*
"Canfield House"	*Demolished in 1999 by order of Mayor*
"Obstruction of Justice House"	*Destroyed by fire in May 2013*
"House of Soul"	*Destroyed by fire in Nov 2013*
"Penny House"	*Destroyed by fire in Nov 2013*
"War House"	*Destroyed by fire in Nov 2013*
"Clock House"	*Destroyed by fire in Dec 2013*
"Party Animal House"	*Destroyed by fire on Mar 7, 2014*
"Dotty Wotty"	*Inhabited by members of Tyree's family*
"The House that"	*Intact, covered in 384,000 pennies*
"Numbers House"	*Intact, headquarters of the Project*
"House of Words"	*Intact*

PEWABIC POTTERY

Started in 1903, Pewabic Pottery flourished during the Arts and Crafts design boom of the early 20th century. The glazed miracles add splendor to many of the most historic homes and buildings in the city. And today, the founders 'Revelation kilns" are still firing off East Jefferson Street.

- ⊳ Fisher Building
- ⊳ Old Main, Wayne State
- ⊳ Guardian Building
- ⊳ Most Holy Redeemer
- ⊳ DMW Airport
- ⊳ Detroit Public Library
- ⊳ Comerica Ballpark
- ⊳ Belle Isle Aquarium
- ⊳ Detroit Police Academy
- ⊳ Cathedral of St. Paul

WATERMELON PARTIES

"The Critic"
August, 1890

Detroit has adopted two new fads in the way of summer entertainments, the barge and watermelon parties. To give a watermelon party, one must provide plenty of melons and some dainty little baskets or boxes to hold the seeds. At the close of the feast, the seeds are counted, and prizes given to the lady and gentleman having the largest number. Barge parties are usually given by young men who wish to entertain their lady friends in some pleasant informal way. The party row around the island in large row boats, and return to the city about ten o'clock where they wind up the evening with a supper. They are very jolly affairs and promise to become very popular especially with the younger crowd.

CADILLAC'S JOURNEY

Cadillac wished to go by way of Lake Erie, but the Governor decreed otherwise. They left the Lachine Rapids the 5th of June, the trees were just budding and game and fish furnished an abundance of food. In July they arrived at Georgian Bay, via the Grand River of the Ottawas, and coasting down the eastern shore of Lake Huron they reached, on the 20th, the river Ste. Claire and the old Fort St. Joseph, at the foot of Lake Huron abandoned by Duluth thirteen years before.

On the 24th of July, 1701, the head of the expedition rounded Belle Isle and soon landed at a little cove at the foot of the present Griswold street. The Ottawas and Hurons, whose villages were near, rushed down to welcome them, as did also a few French "coureurs des bois," who lived here. Two of their names are still preserved: Pierre Roy and Francois Pelletier.

On the following day, with great ceremony, pickets for a new fort on the site of an old stockage were erected and a store house built on the foundation of an abandoned one, previously constructed by the coureurs des bois for their winter supply....Detroit was founded, and its prospects for a successful colony bright.

Legends of Le Detroit, 1884

ON LOCATION

*Film, television and novels
set in the metro area*

- 8 Mile
- Batman vs. Superman
- The Big Bounce
- Bird on a Wire
- Detroit 1-8-7
- Detroit Rock City
- Dreamgirls
- Four Brothers
- Freaks and Geeks
- Gran Torino
- Grosse Pointe Blank
- Hardcore Pawn
- Hoffa
- Home Improvement
- Martin
- Middlesex
- Mr. Paradise
- Out of Sight
- RoboCop [1,2,3]
- The Rosary Murders
- Searching for Sugar Man
- Sister, Sister
- Semi-Pro
- Them
- Tuesdays with Morrie
- Up in the Air
- The Virgin Suicides

THE CHAMBERS BROTHERS

In 1983, four brothers from Marianna, Arkansas, emigrated to Detroit and, in less than five years, turned a nothing drug-dealing scheme into a crack-cocaine empire worthy of a cover story in *TIME* magazine. They were the Chambers — Willie Lee, Billy Joe, Larry and Otis — and they lured teenage foot soldiers from their delta town to run a citywide ring of crack dens, promising "Big City Riches," but ruling the outfit with brutal scare tactics. Business boomed [$3 million a week, at least]. The brothers stockpiled laundry baskets of cash and drove glinting BMWs, a lifestyle of flaunting that was not difficult for police to track. One resident recalls meeting one Chambers' brother at the veterinarian's office on occasion; his two dogs were named Coke and Cane. All four brothers were arrested in February 1988, their five-year comet burning out on national news. Police confiscated $1 million in cash, 68 cars and 250 weapons.

THE LONE RANGER

The "masked crusader" debuted on Detroit's WXYZ radio station on January 30, 1933, the creation of station boss and vaudeville impresario, George Trendle. Trendle had no experience in the saddle, but nonetheless created a cowboy splice of Robin Hood and Zorro, and beat Superman to the punch by five years. His hero, accompanied by his snow-white steed, Silver, the native scout, Tonto [who first appeared in Episode 11] and the triumphant William Tell overture, was beloved by more than 20 million American listeners over nearly 3,000 episodes. A local radio actor was first cast in the title role, and it's rumored that the trademark "Hi Yo, Silver!" line was merely the result of his inability to whistle.

....

OFFICIAL RADIO SHOW INTRODUCTION

A fiery horse with the speed of light, a cloud of dust and a hearty Hi-Yo, Silver! The Lone Ranger, with his faithful Indian companion, Tonto, the daring and resourceful masked rider of the plains led the fight for law and order in the early western United States. Nowhere in the pages of history can one find a greater champion of justice. Return with us now to those thrilling days of yesteryear. From out of the past come the thundering hoofbeats of the great horse Silver! The Lone Ranger rides again!

SANDERS CONFECTIONERY

Halloween Menu, 1935

Kisses	30¢ lb	*Plain Fried Cakes*	25¢ doz
Lolly Pops	2 for 5¢	*Sugared Fried Cakes*	27¢ doz
Owl Stufties	50¢ lb	*Twisted Dough'nts*	25¢ doz
Satinettes	50¢ lb	*Vienna Rolls*	18¢
Spiced Drops	50¢ lb	*Pumpkin Pie*	50¢ each
Cinnamon Potatoes	60¢ lb	*Cheese Straws*	20¢ doz
Marzipan Pum'kns	3 for 10¢	*Mustard*	25¢ jar
Glazed Apples	10¢	*Halloween Pastry*	75¢/1.00

REVIEWS OF NOTE

Artist   *Description... Publication*

Artist	Description... Publication
Aretha Franklin	*We must make do with what we have, and the best female singer we have now is Aretha.* — Rolling Stone, 1969
Bob Seger	*One of the last of a dying breed; unaffected, ungreasebrowed, unhoked-up true-born disciple of rock and roll. But I also feel this boy is lazy.* — CREEM, 1973
Eminem	*Exceptionally witty and musical, discernibly thoughtful and good-hearted, indubitably dangerous and full of shit.* — Village Voice, 2000
Madonna	*She doesn't have the power or range of, say, Cyndi Lauper, but she knows what works on the dance floor.* — Rolling Stone, 1985
MC5	*Just underneath the surface, you can feel the real grain, and it's rough. Run your hands over the MC5, and you get splinters.* — Village Voice, 1968
The Jackson 5	*Given any kind of decent material at all, the Jackson Five should be able to give up many years of good, tight music.* — Rolling Stone, 1970

DEVIL'S NIGHT

The 1970s saw continued population decline, rising crime and neighborhood blight, all boiling up in a scary new tradition on Halloween, which annually evolved into a chaos of deadly arsons, earning the moniker Devil's Night. In 1984, over 800 fires were set on Halloween, most in the city's most abandoned areas. In 1995, Mayor Dennis Archer organized a response, which he called Angel's Night, where citizens took a resolute stand against the terror-ridden night. Law enforcement agencies patrolled and city residents walked their streets to support the efforts, playing all-night watchdog to vacant homes that were especially at risk. Last October, more than 40,000 locals volunteered.

CASS TECHNICAL HIGH SCHOOL

Notable graduates from the esteemed Midtown magnet school

Alumni	Vocation
"Big Sean" Anderson	*Hip-Hop artist*
Kenny Burrell	*Jazz guitarist*
Ellen Burstyn	*Actress, Oscar winner*
Donald Byrd	*Trumpeter*
Paul Chambers	*Jazz bassist*
Alice Coltrane	*Harpist*
Muriel Costa-Greenspan	*Opera singer*
Carole Gist	*Miss USA, 1990*
David Alan Grier	*Comedic actor*
Kwame Kilpatrick	*Former Detroit mayor*
John De Lorean	*DeLorean auto executive*
Howard McGhee	*Bebop trumpeter*
Daniel Okrent	*The New York Times editor*
Della Reese	*Gospel singer, actress*
Diana Ross	*Legendary singer*
Eddie Tolan	*Gold-medal sprinter*
Lily Tomlin	*Actress*
Jack White	*Rock musician*

CONEY ISLANDS

Detroit's trademark [and ubiquitous] lunch to-go, started in the early 1900's by entrepreneurial Greek brothers, Bill and Gus Keros

American	Colombo's	Oscar's
LaFayette	A-Eagle's	Hollywood
Duly's	Gratiot Grill	Caesar's
RedHots	Aloha	Michigan
Zef's	Onasis	L. George's
Zeff's	Aurora	8 Mile Grill
Coney Time	Universal	Capital
The Coney Man	Cosmos	Coney Town
Mike's	Galaxy	Al Raayan
Pete's Grill	Adi's	Detroit One

RIOTS OF 1967

*The following column appeared in dozens of U.S.
newspapers the day after the 12th Street riot in 1967.
It's reprinted, unedited, here.*

[EDITOR'S NOTE:
*UPI reporter Sandra
West, a Negro, has lived
for 13 years just two
blocks from where the
Sunday's riot broke out.
In the following dispatch
she tells us what hap-
pened to her neighborhood
and to her neighbors.*]

"REPORTER
DESCRIBES RIOTS"

Monday, July 24, 1967
By Sandra West

DETROIT [UPI] — Negroes
moved into Detroit's near west
side because it was "a nice neighborhood."

Sunday they cried with fear
as burning and looting raged all
around them.

I have lived in the area with
my parents since 1954.

Sunday I saw sights I never
dreamed possible. I saw things I
had only read about or seen on
television.

Raging fires burned out of
control for blocks and blocks.
Thick black smoke and cinders
rained down at times so heavily
they blocked out homes as close
as 20 feet away.

Looters drove pickup trucks
loaded with everything from
floor mops to new furniture.
Price tags dangled from the mer-
chandise.

Youngsters no more than 8 or
9 years old rode two on a bicycle
with loot stuck under their shirts
and clutched in their arms.

There was agony on the faces
of those who lived close to the
burnings, afraid their homes
would be burned too.

Friends of ours, in and out
of the area, set up telephone
relay systems with us to pass on
any new information. Rumors
spread fast and it was had to
know what was true.

By 5 p.m. it was necessary
to close our home to keep the
smoke from saturating the
house.

By 6:30 p.m. the electricity
went out. We couldn't use our
electric fan and were forced to
open the house again.

We walked to 12th Street where the riots began. There we watched as arsonists touched off fires at two establishments. Burglar alarms wailed. They went unanswered. Negro-owned stores sported hastily printed signs that read "soul brother."

A 12-year-old boy flashed a diamond ring he said he found on his lawn.

On Linwood Avenue, three blocks west of 12th, smoke was so thick it was impossible to see a block away. Some of the families on the blocks between 12th and Linwood packed their belongings and prepared to leave during the night if it became necessary. We were one of those families.

At the height of the rampage, several homes caught fire from the burning stores.

A man, his wife and two small children, stumbled along the street with a suitcase and a bedsheet filled with the few belongings they could grab. Fire had destroyed their home. Tears streamed down the mother's face.

By the 9 p.m. curfew, the streets were relatively quiet, but fear remained etched on the faces of those of us who had to spend the night here.

Nothing stirred on the streets at 10 p.m. except an occasional police car and jeeps and trucks loaded with National Guardsmen. But the residents of "this nice neighborhood" were afraid that the riot was over.

And it wasn't.

COLORED VIGILANT COMMITTEE

Founded in 1843, this underground group aided 15,000 freedom seekers before the Emancipation Proclamation. Below, part of a speech given by founder, William Lambert.

Thus have the committee learned from the past transactions of our people, as well as from history, that the spirit of physical conquest, led on by ignorance, was always formed in enmity, pursued in hatred, inflamed by passion, and consummated in riot and bloodshed, and often without accomplishing the object of its design. The object of of the committee was to lay the foundation for the triumph of the just principles of liberty, and the right of all men to enjoy an equal protection, under the government in which they live, to be done under the dominion of calm and deliberate reason, moral and political warfare.

THE LONDON CHOP HOUSE

Dinner Specials
Saturday, April 6, 1940

APPETIZERS

Gruber's Relish Bowl 35	Ripe Olives 30
1/2 doz. Bluepoints 40	Tomato Juice 20
Fresh Shrimp Cocktail 40	Pineapple or Grapefruit Juice 25
Caviar Canape 90	Radishes 20
Fruit Cocktail 35	Roquefort Stuffed Celery 75
Crabmeat Cocktail 45	Bismarck Herring 35
Marinated Herring 40	Celery 30

[All orders include Today's Soup or Tomato Juice, Potatoes
and Vegetable du Jour — Rolls and Butter]

SOUPS

Ox Tail Soup 15	Onion Soup au Gratin 35; *Cup* 25
[Soup with Bread and Butter 25]	Oyster Stew 50
Genuine Turtle Soup 30; *Cup* 20	Half and Half 60; *with Cream* 70

FISH

Fried Michigan Smelts, Tarter Sauce 75
Boneless Perch Fried in Butter 75
Broiled Superior Whitefish 85
Fried Scallops, Tartar Sauce... 85
Steamed Finnan Haddie, Drawn Butter [15 Minutes........................... 85
Broiled Lake Trout 85
Frog Legs, Road House Style, Cole Slaw and Tartar Sauce 1.00
Whole Broiled Lobster, Julienne Potatoes..1.75

ENTREES

Roast Prime Ribs of Beer.. 90; Extra Cut 1.25
Roast Stuffed Long Island Duckling, Apple Sauce............................... 80
Broiled Hamburger Steak, Mushrooms or Onions 75
Fried Calf's Liver with Bacon... 85
Boiled Smoked Beef Tongue, Fresh Spinach.. 75
Half Fried Spring Chicken, with Combination Salad........................ 1.00
Broiled Pork Tenderloin, Apple Sauce....................................... 85

COLD PLATES

Stuffed Tomatoes with Chicken Salad...................................... 75
1/2 Cold Lobster, Head Lettuce and Mayonnaise................................ 85

SPLIT OF
IMPORTED GRAVES SAUTERNE
OR CHABLIS WINE, 75c

BEVERAGES

Coffee 10   Demi-Tasse 10   Pot of Tea 10

Buttermilk 10   Milk 10

TRY A TALL SENSATIONAL

ZOMBI

World's Most Potent Potion
[Only Two to a Customer Please]
$1.25

WE MAKE NO SUBSTITUTIONS

DIEGO RIVERA

Mexican muralist Diego Rivera spent eleven months in Detroit during 1932 and 1933, commissioned by Edsel Ford, the son of Henry Ford, to paint a large-scale mural at the Institute of Arts. After months observing life at the River Rouge factories, the artist completed a 27-panel fresco that offered homage and critique to modern industry. Quickly, rumors of blasphemy spread through the city, stirring white-hot debate. The city council even called for the murals to be destroyed. DIA Director William Valentiner, in response, said this: "I am thoroughly convinced the day will come when Detroit will be proud to have this work in its midst." Arts Commissioner Albert Kahn remarked: "There is nothing new in these attacks by churchmen. Rembrandt was just as guilty of charges of sacrilege as Rivera. But who throws stones at Rembrandt today?" Rivera meanwhile, leaving the city with Frida Kahlo, called the murals his greatest achievement. Here, a few examples of the spirited commentary.

Detroit Times
October 23, 1932
"From what is already on the walls, the work in material, manner, and enormity is beyond the conception of the people outside the red drapes that cover the finished portions of the wall. When they see it, it will hit them like a bolt."

....

Detroit News
March 18, 1933
"[The murals are] coarse in conception...foolishly vulgar...without meaning for the intelligent observer....a slander to Detroit workingmen...un-American."

....

Detroit Free Press
March 23, 1933
"It is easy to understand the concern and disgust over the grotesquerie and even blasphemy in the Diego Rivera murals...Undoubtedly they contain communist propaganda...The murals certainly cannot be taken seriously. But they might be kept as a historical curiosity — an example of the shallow thinking which was prevalent in this country."

TY COBB

In his decorated career, Detroit Tigers centerfielder
Ty Cobb set 90 Major League records. Many still stand today,
including his .367 lifetime average, his 12 batting titles and his
2,245 runs scored. He was a city icon, living in the middle-class
Woodbridge neighborhood, often walking his dogs on game days
down Trumbull Avenue to the ballpark. In 1936, when the
Hall of Fame had its inaugural vote, Cobb topped all
eligible players in votes, including Babe Ruth.

Nov 19, 1947

Dear "Babe"-

Enclosed find releases signed as you requested, of course "Babe" whatever you would want it's a pleasure to me. I was much pleased to see you in New York and honored that Tris and I could pose with you, from papers I had gathered that you was not so well, well old boy you surprised me in how good you looked. Keep the old chin up boy. Now old pal am going to tell you a little secret kept from you for many years, in my heart and mind I have always admired your ability because you were God given great powers and were always a great ball player, never made many mistakes, never many times threw to wrong spot, also fielded well…that is the story "Babe" "old boy" so now you have it.

I tried from the field to see your wife as I saw from the direction you came only wanted to gesture a greeting kindly tell her of this and kindest regards to her.

By the way "Babe" I would like so much to have a picture of you Tris & I, you are there and in position to secure one for me, won't you send me one.

Yours,

Sincerely,

Ty

FORD'S ASSEMBLY LINE

Excerpted from My Life and Work by Henry Ford, 1922

A Ford car contains about five thousand parts — that is counting screws, nuts, and all. Some of the parts are fairly bulky and others are almost the size of watch parts. In our first assembling we simply started to put a car together at a spot on the floor and workmen brought to it the parts as they were needed in exactly the same way that one builds a house…The first step forward in assembly came when we began taking the work to the men instead of the men to the work. We now have two general principles in all operations — that a man shall never have to take more than one step, if possible it can be avoided, and that no man need ever stoop over.

....

THE PRINCIPLES OF ASSEMBLY ARE THESE:

(1) Place the tools and the men in the sequence of the operation so that each component part shall travel the least possible distance while in the process of finishing.

(2) Use work slides or some other form of carrier so that when a workman completes his operation, he drops the part always in the same place — which place must always be the most convenient place to his hand — and if possible have gravity carry the part to the next workman for his operation.

(3) Use sliding assembly lines by which the parts to be assembled are delivered at convenient distances.

....

The net result of the application of these principles is the reduction of the necessity for thought on the part of the worker and the reduction of his movements to a minimum. He does as nearly as possible one thing with only one movement.

TREATY OF DETROIT

1807

Articles of a treaty made at Detroit, this seventeenth day of November, in the year of our Lord, one thousand eight hundred and seven, by William Hull, governor of the territory of Michigan, with the several nations of Indians, north west of the river Ohio, on the one part, and the sachems, chiefs, and warriors of the Ottoway, Chippeway, Wyandotte, and Pottawatamie nations of Indians, on the other part. To confirm and perpetuate the friendship, which happily subsists between the United States and the nations aforesaid, to manifest the sincerity of that friendship, and to settle arrangements mutually beneficial to the parties.

The sachems, chiefs, and warriors of the nations aforesaid, in consideration of money and goods...do in behalf of their nations hereby cede, relinquish, and forever quit claim, unto the said United States, all right, title, and interest, which the said nations now have, or claim, or ever had, or claimed, in, or unto, the lands comprehended within the following described lines and boundaries: Beginning at the mouth of the Miami river of the lakes, and running thence up the middle thereof, to the mouth of the great Au Glaize river, thence running due north, until it intersects a parallel of latitude, to be drawn from the outlet of lake Huron...following the said boundary line, down said lake, through river Sinclair, lake St. Clair, and the river Detroit, into lake Erie, to a point due east of the aforesaid Miami river, thence west to the place of beginning.

It is hereby stipulated and agreed on that there shall be paid to the said nations, at Detroit, ten thousand dollars, in money, goods, implements of husbandry, or domestic animals...It is further agreed and stipulated, that the said Indian nations shall enjoy the privilege of hunting and fishing on the lands ceded as aforesaid, as long as they remain the property of the United States.

MALCOLM X

In 1963, Malcolm X gave perhaps his most controversial speech, calling out the black bourgeois and criticizing what he deemed a spineless March on Washington. "Everyone of those Toms was out of town by sundown," he told the attendees at King Solomon Baptist Church on 14th Street. Four months later, he would leave the Nation of Islam.

"MESSAGE TO THE GRASS ROOTS"
November 10, 1963
Detroit, Michigan

You don't have a peaceful revolution. You don't have a turn-the-other-cheek revolution. There's no such thing as a nonviolent revolution. The only kind of revolution that's nonviolent is the Negro revolution. The only revolution based on loving your enemy is the Negro revolution. ... Revolution is bloody, revolution is hostile, revolution knows no compromise, revolution overturns and destroys everything that gets in its way. And you, sitting around here like a knot on the wall, saying, "I'm going to love these folks no matter how much they hate me." No, you need a revolution. Whoever heard of a revolution where they lock arms, singing "We Shall Overcome"? You don't do that in a revolution. You don't do any singing, you're too busy swinging.

THE FUR TRADE

In Fred C. Camil's 1951 book, When Beaver Was King, *the historian describes the decades of commerce [often unscrupulous] between European settlers and Native tribes. Below, a list of prized trade items for furs.*

- Strouds [blankets] of blue, black and scarlet
- Heavy napped woolen cloth
- Worsted and yarn hose
- Flowered serges
- Calicos and calamancos
- Ribbons of all sorts
- Threads, needles, and awls
- Beaver and fox traps
- Stone and plain rings
- Horn combs, scissors, razors, and hand mirrors
- Brass and tin kettles
- Tobacco, pipes, and snuff
- Tomahawks and hatchets
- Black and white wampum
- Red leather trunks
- Pewter spoons and gilt cups

THE PURPLE GANG

Detroit outlawed booze a year before the federal government, and by 1929, bootlegging was the city's second largest industry behind automobiles. The Purple Gang, started by four brothers from the paradise Valley neighborhood, ran a viciously successful operation, hijacking other Canadian rumrunners and using so savage a brand of turf warring that Al Capone chose to work with them, not against. The Purples were even rumored to be behind the Lindbergh baby kidnapping. In the early 1930's, Sicilian rivals, inter-gang strife and renewed police courage broke up the Purple syndicate. Most members were murdered, put in prison or never heard from again.

SPEAKEASIES OF NOTE

Club Dexter	The Rathskeller
Club Forest	The Par Four Club
The Castle	Green Tree Club
Dexter Chop House	Club 46
The Rialto	Little Harry
The Studio	Club Piccadilly
Pioneer Bridge Club	The Mayfield Club

THE ELECTRIFYING MOJO

Before XM and MTV, there was Detroit's Midnight Funk Association, a 1980s radio brethren led by a mysterious local DJ called the Electrifying Mojo. Part Star Wars, part Soul Train, Mojo's late night programming, found on the far right turn of the dial, was an urban blend of soul, New Wave, hip hip's precursors and emerging techno. Kraftwerk, Rick James and the B-52's were favorites. Many even claim he discovered Prince. And every evening at midnight, Planet Mojo honked horns and flashed lights in allegiance. Beyond radio as a high art, Mojo's broadcasts were a practice in solidarity.

ELMORE LEONARD

The famed crime noir genius, affectionately tabbed as the "Dickens of Detroit," published over 50 books and screenplays before his death in 2013. Below are his rules for writing.

① Never open a book with weather.

② Avoid prologues.

③ Never use a verb other than "said" to carry dialogue.

④ Never use an adverb to modify the verb "said."

⑤ Keep your exclamation points under control.

⑥ Never use the words "suddenly" or "all hell broke loose."

⑦ Use regional dialect, patois, sparingly.

⑧ Avoid detailed descriptions of characters.

⑨ Don't go into great detail describing places and things.

⑩ Try to leave out the part that readers tend to skip.

"HOUDINI ILL"
United Press
Famous Magician Fights for Life After Operation

Detroit, Mich., Oct. 26. — Harry Houdini was fighting for his life today and although his physicians reported his condition as "fair," they said the crisis would come in two or three days. The famous magician underwent an operation for appendicitis following his collapse at the end of his performance in a Detroit theater Saturday night. A diagnosis revealed Houdini had given two performances after his appendix had been ruptured. "We have grave doubts for Mr. Houdini's recovery," physicians said. At the completion of his last act Sunday, Houdini stumbled into the arms of an attendant. He had performed with a temperature of 104 degrees.

> *Harry Houdini died from peritonitis at Detroit's Grace Hospital on Halloween, 1926.*

INTERMITTENT WIPERS

United States Patent D 3,351,836
Filed Dec. 1. 1964

Under certain conditions, such as light rain or splashback produced by other vehicles on wet roads, the condition of the windshield is often in what may be termed a wet-dry condition. Continuous windshield wiper operation with such a windshield condition may cause smearing to obscure the vision of the driver. . .The present invention provides an intermittent windshield wiper system which is truly responsive to the condition of the windshield. [excerpt]

Detroit inventor Robert W. Kearns won landmark infringement cases against Ford and Chrysler for his wiper technology, and sparked both a New Yorker *magazine profile and a major motion picture,* Flash of Genius.

HOCKEYTOWN

The Detroit Red Wings have won the most Stanley Cup championships of any NHL franchise based in the United States. First organized in 1926, the Red Wings were one of the Original Six, the first sextet of teams to make up the National Hockey League. The team holds the longest current streak of consecutive playoff appearances in all of pro sports at 23 years.

Stanley Cup	Losing Team	Captain
1936	Toronto Maple Leafs	*Doug Young*
1937	New York Rangers	*Doug Young*
1943	Boston Bruins	*Sid Abel*
1950	New York Rangers	*Sid Abel*
1952	Montreal Canadiens	*Sid Abel*
1954	Montreal Canadiens	*Ted Lindsay*
1955	Montreal Canadiens	*Ted Lindsay*
1997	Philadelphia Flyers	*Steve Yzerman*
1998	Washington Capitols	*Steve Yzerman*
2001	Carolina Hurricanes	*Steve Yzerman*
2008	Pittsburgh Penguins	*Nicklas Lidstrom*

MAPS

*Hand-illustrated maps to tell stories about historic
architecture, dive bars, hit records, the art world,
Eastern Market, and the future of Detroit*

The Fisher

Boston-Edison

Book Tower

Michigan Central Station

Lafayette
Park

The
Guardian

Belle Isle
Conservatory

≫ ARCHITECTURE ≪

*Booming manufacturing brought iconic towers and
inspiring home design, now mixed with city blight.*

FISHER BUILDING

The auto barons handed the
creative keys to architect Albert
Kahn for this 441-foot New
Center tower. Exhibit A: 40
kinds of marble in the three-
story lobby. 3011 *W Grand Blvd*

BOSTON-EDISON

Historic neighborhood in city
center, home to Joe Louis and
Berry Gordy, governors and
car kings, who all built grand
10,000-square-foot Tudor man-
sions and Italian villas.

BOOK TOWER

In the 1920s, three brothers
built both the Book Cadillac
Hotel, restored in 2008, and the
Book Tower, an Italian Renais-
sance topic of debate. Note the
freakishly tall fire escape. 1265
Washington Blvd

MICHIGAN CENTRAL STATION

The city's monument to soaring
ruin, this grandiose depot in Corktown saw 200 trains a day at its
height. The final Chicago-bound
departure in 1988. 2001 *15th St*

BELLE ISLE CONSERVATORY

Modeled after Monticello, the
85-foot glass dome structure is
the jewel of Belle Isle, housing a
rose garden, fernery and a collection of orchids rescued during
World War II.

GUARDIAN BUILDING

A downtown monument to
Art Deco, ornamented with
Mankato stone, orange brick
and tens of thousands of locally-
fired Pewabic tiles, glazed and
mosaicked in the Aztec spirit.
500 *Griswold St*

LAFAYETTE PARK

On 78 acres east of downtown,
Ludwig Mies Van Der Rohe
left his mark on Detroit, seen in
strict-lined, glass-and-aluminum
townhomes [186 total] and two
modern apartment towers.

LOCAL EXPERTS *Founded by writer-researcher Dan Austin,
HistoricDetroit.org is a well of city stories about classic buildings
and architects, many long gone. Worth bookmarking.*

⫸ NEIGHBORHOOD BARS ⫷

*Raise a glass to six iconic [if rickety] Detroit bars, classics
that will make you want to live around the corner.*

ABICK'S

Ninety years young, matron
Manya Abick Soviack was born
upstairs at this dive-hunter
dream. Soak in the chili pot-
cigar smoke aromas and bask
in the Tiffany glass glow. *3500
Gilbert St*

....

TEMPLE BAR

The southern gateway into
Cass Corridor, this gay-friendly
anchor buzzes in a steady stream
of all kinds — greeted first by
Jameson the house pup, then
by a legendary disco ball that
still spins Haute to Death dance
parties. *2906 Cass Ave*

....

RAVEN LOUNGE

Not much to applaud in this
blighted area, but the Raven's
legendary soul and R&B
lineups keep audiences coming
strong Thursday through
Saturday nights. It's a $5 cover
most evenings. *5145 Chene*,
313-924-7133

TWO-WAY INN

Onetime brothel, dancehall,
village jail and dentist's office,
this corner spot now raises $2
Stroh's to the ghost of Colonel
Philetus Norris, the original
builder of the rickety building. *17897 Mount Elliott St,
2wayinn.com*

....

BRONX BAR

Forget peanuts, the Bronx
used to give out free bacon.
Thought that tradition is
dead, the two-handed burgers
are legit and the pool table is
perfectly moody. This Cass
Corridor dive a Detroit staple.
4476 2nd Ave

....

TOM'S TAVERN

Sleepy [and slanted] west
side housebar tapes a paper
sack clock to the wall [always
11:15], celebrates Babe Ruth
once a year. Still standing after
break-ins, car crashes and long
winters. *10093 W 7 Mile*

LOCAL EXPERT *New icon of crafted cocktails, the Sugar House on
Corktown Row channels a speakeasy-era of fancy concoctions and
brassy, dim-lit digs. 2130 Michigan Ave, sugarhousedetroit.com*

TOM'S TAVERN

7he BRONX

ABICK'S

M10

WYOMING

SEVEN MILE

BAR

M5

PRENTIS

SECOND

96

M12

94

DENNIS

GILBERT

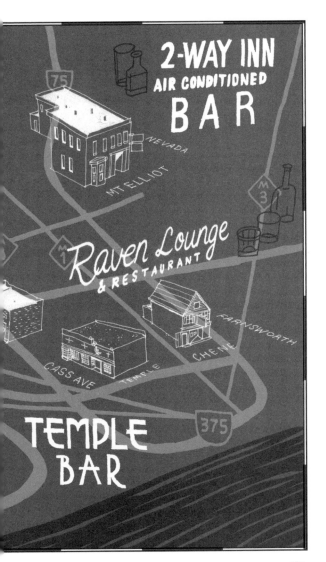

2-WAY INN
AIR CONDITIONED
BAR

75

NEVADA

MT ELLIOT

M 3

Raven Lounge
& RESTAURANT

MT

FARNSWORTH

CHENE

CASS AVE

TEMPLE

375

TEMPLE
BAR

⫸ HIT RECORDS ⫷

*From the legendary Motown sound to the Stooge-MC5 punks
to early techno, Detroit spans the music spectrum.*

THE SUPREMES

Motown writers Holland-Dozier-Holland, the Funk Brothers and the velvety-voiced trio brought "Baby Love" into the world in 1964, one of five straight number ones.

....

MC5

Rolling Stone put the early punk crew on their cover for "Kick Out the Jams," a hollering rebel's rant recorded live at Detroit's Grande Ballroom on Halloween night, 1968.

....

J DILLA

The east side producer [Common, A Tribe Called Quest and The Roots] left behind a serious rap catalogue of his own when he died in 2006, including "So Far To Go" from *The Shining*.

....

JOHN LEE HOOKER

The Delta blues legend worked in Ford factories before his music took off with "Boogie Chillen'," a legendary riff recorded in three takes at United Sound studios in 1948.

....

BILL HALEY AND HIS COMETS

Released in 1954, Highland Park-born Haley's rendition of the "Rock Around the Clock" ushered in the 50s rock era and was later used as the TV theme song for *Happy Days*.

....

BOB SEGER

The heartland rocker fronted numerous Detroit bands in the 60s and 70s, but rode to stardom later with hits like "Night Moves" and "Like a Rock," the Chevy truck anthem.

....

ARETHA FRANKLIN

Daughter of famous Detroit minister, C.L Franklin, the Queen's career truly took off with her album, *I Never Loved a Man the Way I Love You*, which featured the unforgettably catchy single, "Respect."

LOCAL EXPERT *Vinyl lovers should stop in Hello Records in Corktown and Peoples Records on Woodward Avenue in Midtown — both will gladly dig deep into the history of Detroit sound.*

⫸ ARTS ⫷

*Wide open spaces, cheap rent and cultural complexities
make Detroit a haven for all kinds of art projects.*

DETROIT INSTITUTE OF ARTS
Opened during the Post-WWI
industry boom, 100 galleries
strong. Best bets: Degas,
Cézanne and Diego Rivera's
iconic ode to-critique of the
auto industry. *dia.org*
....

MOCAD
Raw and cavernous space that
used to be an auto showroom
transformed into exhibition
and public performance venue.
Love the Monster Drawing
Rallies. 4454 *Woodward Ave,*
mocadetroit.org
....

WHAT PIPELINE
Saturdays-only space in
Southwest, created for smaller
art pop-ups, solo shows and a
refreshing penchant towards
international works. 3525 *W*
Vernor, whatpipeline.com
....

PUBLIC POOL
This co-op champions the city's
contemporary scene with artists'

lectures, informal gatherings,
off-the-radar shows and a real
sense of rebellion. 3309 *Caniff,*
apublicpool.com
....

HAMTRAMCK DISNEYLAND
Former GM assemblyman's
messy backyard masterpiece is
a teetering collection of lawn
ornaments, wind-powered
ducks, with Ukrainian folk
music. 12087 *Klinger St, the alley*
....

HEIDELBERG PROJECT
Begun in 1986, some of the two
blocks of whimsy and protest,
envisioned by Tyree Guyton on
the east side, have been burned
down or bulldozed. *heidelberg.org*
....

MBADS AFRICAN BEAD MUSEUM
Olayami Dabls' rowhouse of
African sculptures, pottery and
ceremonial beads, some dating
back 400 years. The exterior is a
sight in itself, wallpapered in bright
patterns and African motifs.
6559 *Grand River Ave, mbad.org*

LOCAL EXPERT *Trinosophes in Eastern Market is part coffeehouse, part
concert venue with a side of book stall and airy gallery space. Art lovers,
this is your hang. 1464 Gratiot Ave, trinosophes.com*

DISNEYLAND
This wy FOR
ViSiTO R. ..

PUBLIC
POOL

HAMTRAMCK

THE DETROIT INSTITUTE ARTS

DIA

DABL'S
GALLERY

Warren Ave.

MUSE
DIST

W. Grand Blvd.

MBAD
AFRICAN BEAD MUSEUM

THE
HEIDELBERG
PROJECT

and Blvd.

TRINOSOPHES

Gratiot Ave.

CONTEMPORARY ART DETROIT

MOCAD

Woodward Ave

River Ave

⋙ EASTERN MARKET ⋘

A few favorites that surround America's oldest public marketplace, the heartbeat of a Motor City Saturday.

DEVRIES & CO.

Formerly known as R. Hirt Jr. & Co., this European grocer meets Midwest deli is meat and cheese heaven, selling wedges of French brie alongside Mason jars of Michigan hot sauce. *2468 Market Street, 313-568-7777*

....

SUPINO PIZZERIA

Chief pizza-tosser Dave Mancini opened this new institution in 2008, and we're ever-grateful: his massive pies are arguably the best in town. [We love you too Buddy's!] Try the garlic-ricottta namesake. *2457 Russell St., supinopizzeria.com*

....

BUSY BEE HARDWARE

The handyman's hangout. Established in 1918, this fix-it-up store is more than just a place to buy nails: the staff will both advise your home improvement purchases and shoot the breeze all afternoon. *1401 Gratiot Ave.,* 313-567-0785

BERT'S MARKETPLACE

Soul food and Motown karaoke, anyone? Bert Dearing's lively jazz and blues bar is the definition of laid-back cool [served with a side of collard greens]. *2727 Russell St., bertsentertainmentcomplex.com*

....

LOVE'S CUSTARD PIE

Southern delicacies migrated up north with the Love family, whose specialty chess pie is crackly crème brulee-like on top with gooey butter filling. Me oh my. *10040 W. McNichols Rd., lovescustardpies.com*

....

MURALS

In 1969, architect Alex Pollock commissioned a series of brightly-colored murals, and in the decades since, they've endured the winter cold and spurred on other grafitti'd displays of affection. Check walls of Eastern Market Cold Storage and Cost Plus wine.

LOCAL EXPERTS *Load up on Mitten State stuff like Carhartt and Detroit Denim at Detroit Mercantile, a firehouse turned modern general store. 3434 Russell St, detroitmercantile.com*

⫸ FUTURE ⫷

With co-working initiatives, tech start-ups and endless creative opportunities, optimism and ideas lead Detroit's way forward.

GREEN GARAGE
Housed in a former Model T showroom, Tom and Peggy Brennan's gorgeously reclaimed incubator and co-working hub focuses on the sustainable future and champions triple-bottom-line enterprises. Check out the brown bag lunches. *4444 Second Ave, greengarage-detroit.com*

DETROIT LABS
Daydreamers who deliver: an app-focused tech start-up for the people, including platforms for mobile fundraising, loan management and a landmark tracker. *detroitlabs.com*

WRITE-A-HOUSE
Equal parts literary and neighborhood boost, this non-profit buys neglected homes in anchor communities, renovates them, then deeds each house to a working writer via an annual essay contest. *writeahouse.org*

COLLEGE FOR CREATIVE STUDIES
CCS is world-renowned for creative thinkers, most especially for innovative transportation design. CCS also houses the Henry Ford Academy, an art-design charter school for middle and high school students. *460 West Baltimore, collegeforcreativestudies.edu*

LOVELAND
Silicon Valley meets Motor City. These techies create an easy-to-use digital database of public property information, "blexting" [text images and updates about blight] to create a real-time map of modern Detroit. *1514 Washington Blvd, makeloveland.com*

RED BULL HOUSE OF ART
Industrial space for Michigan artists studios and inspiring lower gallery space, lit with neon and stocked with energy drinks. *1551 Winder St*

LOCAL EXPERTS *TechTown is Detroit's font of new enterprise. It opened shop in 2000 [in a former GM facility] with the specific purpose of accelerating businesses that put Detroit back on the map. techtowndetroit.org*

CCS

SHINOLA
COLLEGE FOR CREATIVE ST

WOODWARD AVE

Green
Garag

BUSINESS INCUBA

MICHIGAN AVE

Ponyride

DETROIT DENIM
SMITH SHOP
HERITAGE WORKS
ORDER & OTHER

THE EMPOWERMENT PLAN
BEEHIVE RECORDING
ANTHOLOGY COFFEE
THE DIRT LABEL

INTERVIEWS

Fifteen conversations with locals of note about urban planning, Motown, the priesthood, driving a bus, running a barbershop, writing poems and more

⫸ NAOMI LONG MADGETT ⫷

POET LAUREATE

I GOT ENGAGED by mail because my first husband was still in the army.

WE DIDN'T EVEN have time for a wedding reception because we had to catch the train to Detroit.

WE COULDN'T eat at some restaurants or stay in some hotels. I didn't expect that here.

THERE ARE GOOD and bad people in all races. I went through prejudice so early in my life, that I couldn't let that consume me.

IT SEEMS STRANGE to be 90 years old. I still can't imagine it, but I did have a great party.

MY FIRST POEM was published by a daily newspaper in Virginia when I was 13.

I MET Langston Hughes when I was at Virginia State College, and I timidly gave him a looseleaf notebook of my poems. And in the middle of his reading, he read several of mine.

HE HAD READ the whole thing and penciled comments.

PEOPLE THINK there's something sacrosanct about spontaneity. Poems don't come out perfect the first time.

IF IT COMES on like a caveman, if it drags me by the hair, then I'll write it.

A DRY PERIOD is when nothing comes. When I do start writing again, there's something different.

IF A LINE comes to me in bed, I don't dare wait until morning. I turn the lamp on, then another line comes, turn it off, turn it back on.

THERE'S SO MUCH subconscious in poetry.

MY MOST POPULAR poem is "Midway." I've come this far to freedom and I won't turn back / I'm climbing to the highway from my old dirt track.

EVERYBODY LIKES it but me.

⟫⟫ FRANCIS GRUNOW ⟪⟪

URBANIST

I WENT TO Columbia University to study cities.

IT'S NOT ABOUT good planning or bad planning. You can have all the rules you want, but it's about inspiring people and changing hearts.

I THOUGHT we could just plan Detroit back.

A WAR WASN'T waged here. It's not like Katrina happened. Aliens didn't come down and do this.

SO WHO did this?

PEOPLE WANT a single answer.

CHINA IS A version of Detroit 100 years ago.

MY GRANDFATHER worked with Ford for 50 years. He was an orphan from Germany and Ford was his father, his school, his career, his social network.

I FELT FREER in New York without a car.

HUDSON'S Department Store. That one stung.

IT WAS 2.2 million square feet. Red brick. More switchboards than any building outside the Pentagon. Seventy elevators.

IT WAS THE largest building to ever be imploded at the time.

WE CALL THEM the death fences.

IT REALLY IS the best and worst of times.

THE AMOUNT of people that I don't know at a party makes me happy. I find it hopeful.

CITIES ARE MADE for transactions. For me to be next to you. That's the bad thing about a car.

ROME. LONDON. These places don't go away.

A GOOD neighbor is someone who knows enough to care. It's someone you share your story with. A neighbor is in it with you.

⫸ DREAM HAMPTON ⫷

WRITER AND FILMMAKER

I WAS BORN in area called the Blackbottom.

MY MOM WAS a waitress and my dad was a mechanic.

IT WASN'T UNTIL Cass Tech that I realized there were people out there with more money than us.

CASS TECH was an oasis.

AERODYNAMICS. Fashion Design. Jazz. Chemistry. It was like college filled with the most talented high school kids in the city.

THERE'D ALWAYS been a coastal pull.

THE SECOND FLIGHT from Detroit was the Black Flight. It was the black working class, and it was devastating.

WHITE FLIGHT had been about fear. Black Flight was about a lack of services.

DETROIT AT ONE point had more black homeowners than any city in America.

IT'S NOT JUST white people imagining it. It actually happens. Institutions actually devalue black neighborhoods.

THE CITY WAS being mismanaged. Banks had a chokehold on us. And the billion-dollar crack industry set our streets on fire.

WHEN I THINK of Detroit, I think of blackness and brilliance and adaptability.

IN GROSSE POINT today, there are five or six Kroger's in a five-mile area. But there are none inside the city of Detroit.

IN 2008, my dad died. He had a heart attack and the ambulance took 27 minutes to get to their house.

SO I MOVED home.

WHEN I GOT there I saw gardens. Urban farms. More than anywhere else in America. And my daughter didn't want to leave.

⫸ WILLIE FORTUNE ⫷

PROFESSIONAL BOXER

I WAS BORN AND RAISED in D, on the west side of Seven Mile. My great grandmother moved to Detroit from Georgia.

COMING FROM a family of women, people always trying you. They think you soft.

MY VERY FIRST FIGHT was out of the gym. We had neighborhood front yard boxing. It kept us out of trouble.

MY FATHER WAS an amateur and my uncle turned pro when I was a kid, so I was always around world-class fighters. The doors of the world opened through the door of boxing.

I HAD A pretty good warehouse job until the economy started getting bad. That's when I started.

IS 25 YEARS old late? That's what a lot of people say.

THEY LAUGHED at me. I was 225 pounds, but now I fight at 160.

A LOT OF shadowboxing. And miles and miles and miles of running.

I RUN A LOT in the city. It gives me motivation seeing where I came from.

IT TAKES A very disciplined person to box.

I'M WHAT THEY call "busy." They might hit me with prettier shots, but I'll out work them.

I'LL EXHAUST them.

I TAKE IT ALL IN. To be a fighter, you have to be a thinker.

MOST GUYS get knocked down wanna jumped right back up. The best throw their egos out of the ring.

HARDEST PUNCH I ever took was my first devastating body punch. It paralyzed me. It felt like he reached in and touched my lung. I was down four minutes.

I'VE NEVER been hit like that again.

⇶ MARTHA REEVES ⇷

MOTOWN SINGER

I KNEW I WAS going to be a singer when I was three.

WHEN HE WASN'T working, my dad sang and played Blues guitar.

MY MOTHER TOLD ME in the beginning, she said, "Don't ever sing a song unless you can mean it from your heart. If you can feel it."

YOU REJECT a song if it's against your spirit.

I WAS SINGING at the Twenty Grand, one of the biggest clubs in the city, and an A&R director from Motown walked up and gave me his card.

THE NEXT DAY I quit my job at the dry cleaners, and I went to Motown.

I TOOK A BUS to the west side of Detroit, got off at this house with a hand-painted sign, passed a long line of people at the door and walked right into his office.

HE'D BEEN UP all night writing a song with Marvin Gaye.

THEY ASKED ME to answer telephones.

"MARTHA REEVES, A&R. May I help you?" That went on for three hours.

BERRY GORDY SAYS I snuck in the back door, but I'm telling you I came in the front.

I SANG BACKUP whenever somebody needed a voice. Or if they needed hand claps. We spent a lot of time snapping our fingers.

I MADE $5 a session.

WE WERE AT Berry's Christmas party, me in my little party dress, and the Hollands and Lamont Dozier asked me to come to the studio for a song. It was midwinter, and he sang a song called "Heat Wave."

IMAGINE THAT: Love is like a heat wave, and there was snow on the ground.

WHEN I'M GIVEN a song I have to make it my own. Change lyrics, change melodies, make it my own.

WHEN YOU'RE IN church and the Holy Spirit comes on you, there's a hot feeling there, from the top of your head to the tips of your toes. It's a heat wave.

BERRY'S THING was to discover an act and move on to the next.

YES, it was competitive.

THE FIRST GIRLS group was The Marvalettes. Then we came along. And then The Supremes. It was a chain of success, and it was all about business.

HAD THERE NEVER been a Stevie Wonder, there would have been no Michael Jackson.

I WAS IN the room when they first brought Stevie in. He said, "Hi, I'm Stevie," and I said, "I'm Martha." Then he came to me and said, "You sound like a nice person, let me see what you look like."

HE COULD PLAY anything he put his hands on. I had to restrain him from calling Russia on the telephone.

EIGHT YEARS OLD playing a grand piano. Drums like he'd known Gene Cooper personally. The xylophone, the bongos, a harmonica out of his pocket. Berry stood there and he said, "This child is a wonder."

THE KEY TO Motown was the group of musicians who walked into Studio A everyday.

IT'S BEEN 50 years and over 100 Vandellas.

I SING everyday. It's a muscle. If you have a car, you need to keep it tuned up.

THE TEMPTATIONS or The Supremes or The Four Tops or Stevie Wonder or Gladys Knight or The Marvalettes or Martha and the Vandellas — if someone sees or hears any of the Motown acts, then they've seen all of us. It's universal.

Martha and the Vandellas were one of Motown's most successful groups in the 1960s. The trio scored Billboard hits with "Heat Wave" and "Jimmy Mack," but it was their 1964 single, "Dancin' in the Street," written in part by Marvin Gaye, that secured their place in American music legend. It is one of 50 sound recordings preserved by the Library of Congress.

⫸ FATHER TOM LUMPKIN ⫷

PRIEST

I GREW UP in Detroit. Back then, if you were Catholic and you were a boy and you were interested in God, you almost automatically thought about becoming a priest.

IT WAS THOUGHT that priests should give up everything. Human friendships, human life. You'd flee the world.

CHRISTIANITY IS a very fleshy religion. We have this sense that you find God in stuff.

I ASKED THE Bishop for the job 36 years ago. I had a need to get with poor people. I had this feeling that I was in danger of losing my soul.

WHEN WE'RE AT the soup kitchen, we don't preach. Not with words. And we don't hurry people.

ANOTHER PICTURE of heaven is a mansion. A house with many rooms. Right now, we have nine rooms in Day House. Yes, we're giving the homeless a place, but I think it's more.

THE GOSPEL IS about love and joy. You can also find God in people who are wounded.

I DID A 37-day water fast in 1972 against the Vietnam War.

WHEN YOU DID it to the least of these, you did it for me. The Pope has gotten us back to the essentials.

THE BIG DANGER of affluence is that you get the illusion that you're self-sufficient.

WORKING WITH the poor shows you a shadow side of yourself. I do feel overwhelmed at times.

MY BEST FRIEND is a woman. And, yes, that's been tricky. We have dinner twice a week.

WE COME TO God through other people all the time. It's not a solitary experience. Loneliness is never good.

DETROIT IS A great place to try to live out the gospel.

»» ROBIN EAGAN ««

FIRE MARSHALL

MY SISTER wanted to be a firefighter. And because I was an athlete and in pretty good shape, she asked me to help her train to take the test.

THE DAY OF the test she said, "You're here, so you might as well take the test."

I ENDED UP passing, and I had the best time for any female that did the stair climb.

YOU HAD TO run up five flights of stairs with a tank on your back. I was a runner, so I did well.

WE WERE HIRED on the fire department together, but eight weeks in she quit. She's retiring this year after 33 years with the Postal Service.

WE HAVE AROUND 900 members of the fire service. Eleven are women.

YOU'LL ALWAYS be an outsider in the fire service as a woman.

THE HIGHER you go up, the more difficult it becomes.

YOU'RE THE FIRST person in the department to be pregnant, the first to have a baby. They don't know what to do with you.

I SPENT FOUR and a half years in the fire house. That was enough.

WHEN I FIRST became an inspector, we had 32 people. Now we have eight.

INVESTIGATING FIRES is about cause and origin. I wanted to go out in the field and inspect, where I could be at home every night and the element of danger wouldn't be as bad.

WITH ARSON, we'll find multiple burn sites. Gasoline or some other accelerator fluid that's been used. We have dogs, too.

WE PROBABLY HAVE more arson or suspicious fires than any place in the world——not just the US. The world.

ARSON IS just a symptom.

⫸ AL SOBOTKA ⫷

ZAMBONI OPERATOR

DETROIT HAS HIGH standards for ice.

I STARTED AT Olympic Stadium back in the summer of 1971. I was seventeen.

AFTER TWO SEASONS on nights, and about a year on days, I got to learn to drive the machine, the Zamboni.

GREASE IS THE most important part of taking care of the Zamboni.

I HAD DREAMS about messing up the ice.

MY FIRST PUBLIC resurface job was "Ice Follies." It was nerve wracking.

ICE DOES HAVE to be broken in. It has to be used to be good. It's like an ice cube in your freezer.

YOU EDGE THE ICE, then you dry shave it, then you resurface it. It depends on the night before — sweat and spit, you know.

THE COACH doesn't like any ruts or skate marks, ever.

IT FIRST STARTED in 1952, but I picked up the octopus thing in the 90s. Someone threw an octopus out after the last game. I got it and I gave it a little twirl and people sort of got excited.

WE MADE THE Stanley Cup Finals in 1995. That was octopus heaven there. It was raining octopus.

A LITTLE SLIME got in the other goalie's eyeball.

WHEN WE WEREN'T winning, people called them the Dead Wings.

REFEREES RATE the ice after every game, and the visiting team too. Two games in a row we've come in at 100%.

SOME PEOPLE SAY I'm married to the building and married to the ice. There's some truth to that.

≫ LAKISHKA RAYBON ≪

WATCH ASSEMBLER

BEFORE THIS JOB, I never even wore a watch.

THE ONLY THING I knew about a watch was how to set it. Now the amount I know is mind-blowing.

THEY MADE US take a dexterity test and get timed putting little pieces together. It was intimidating.

I DID IT ALL in under a minute.

BEFORE SHINOLA, I worked at in a factory that made parts for the Big Three.

IT WAS A giant building and it was loud and I'd walk in clean and walk out dirty.

I WAS WITH that company for nine years, and we were bought and sold three times. I was eventually laid off during cutbacks.

IT STRESSED ME out, of course. But I knew that I had to get back on my feet.

WHEN I WAS hired, nobody knew nothing about Shinola.

THE MOVEMENT is what we call the guts of the watch. It's like the engine.

THE LITTLE THINGS are really, really important.

WE HAD TRAINERS come over from Thailand, and they'd spank your hands if you did something wrong.

WHEN YOU ARE quiet, it gives you the chance to really focus.

AT THE END OF the line, we go through a final check. Making sure everything is ticking. Yes, we still listen for the ticking, even with all this technology.

WE MADE OVER 50,000 watches last year.

PEOPLE AREN'T amplifying the good in Detroit, all the positive things that are happening.

THE FUTURE feels limitless.

»» STEPHEN MAGSIG ««

OIL PAINTER

WHEN I WENT back to school for tech illustration, I started working in automotive.

....

I'VE BEEN painting Detroit for twenty years.

....

YOU COULD GO anywhere then. We were pretty adventurous and jumped fences. Nobody would stop you. Now so much is fenced off and patrolled.

....

I'VE HAD HOMELAND security stop me a number of times.

....

THE FACTORIES then were still like they were in the 1940s. I still paint from those photographs.

....

FINDING BEAUTY in this, in decay and industrial subjects, is a challenge. But there is beauty if you look.

....

THE PENOBSCOT Building is one of the most beautiful buildings in Detroit.

....

I THINK PEOPLE would distract from my paintings. Man's mark is there though. The graffiti, the industry. The paintings are about what man has done to our environment.

....

I PAINT in the afternoon, break for dinner, then I paint until at least 11. I used to paint from 2.

....

THOSE OLD habits die hard.

....

NEW YORK IS more vertical, Detroit is more of a horizontal city.

....

YOU CAN LOOK at paintings and tell what time of day or year it is, just by the shadow and the light.

....

I REMEMBER I was shooting a wonderful little liquor store. Group of men asked me what I was doing. And they say, "You have to go over here. There are wonderful houses down here." And I did—that kind of surprises you.

....

SOMEONE TRIED to run me over on Mission Avenue.

....

IT'S A VERY COMPLEX city.

....

SO MANY of the things I've painted are gone now.

⫸ LONZO JACKSON ⫷

BARBER SHOP OWNER

BARBERING IS a good trade. I started when I was eleven years old.

I HAVE THREE older brothers, and they all cut hair—we had a barber shop in our basement.

PEOPLE, THEY LOVE coming to the barber shop—they think, let's talk, let's have fun. A lot of people talk too much.

FIRST PERSON whose hair I cut was a friend of mine—we were in the sixth grade. His name was James, and I really messed him up.

YOU USE SHEARS for white hair, and the buzzer for black hair. None of it's really hard, only cutting white people's hair.

STYLES COME BACK around. It's a full circle. Ball fade, corvallis, taper, taper fade.

THE BARBER THAT owned the shop, he was a beautiful guy—but he wouldn't spend any mon-ey. All he did was pull the chairs in and say, "Next!"

ALL DIFFERENT KINDS of people come in—you'd be surprised.

THIS BLOCK CHANGED a lot over the last ten, fifteen years. There used to be houses on this street. And that factory wasn't here.

THAT'S WHERE I bought my first car, right down there. A 1963 Thunderbird, white. I was 19, and I tore it up in 6 days.

I HAD A regular job for 26 years. It was a margarine distributor.

I WAS THERE until it closed down, and everyone was devastated.

BARBERING CAME right back to me, it's like swimming. It never leaves you.

CUTTING HAIR is in my family. My nephews, my nieces, my daughter.

≫ AMY KAHERL ≪

MICROFINANCE

WHAT CAN YOU DO with a little? In this city, the answer is a lot.

I WAS LIVING in LA and my mom got really sick. I just thought I'd come home for two months, or six months, or a year—no plan. A little bit turned into a long bit.

SOUP IS A micro-granting dinner to fund creative projects in neighborhoods.

WE SIT DOWN at the tables and everyone has four minutes to share an idea. All the money goes into a pot and the winner walks out with it.

SOUP, SALAD, bread and a vote.

SIX MONTHS INTO it SOUP was in *The New York Times*.

THERE ARE SO many beautiful stories already in Detroit, and if we whitewash those and try to say we're starting new, we'll lose our important voices.

I FOUND THIS old wooden vot-ing box, and circle your choice on a strip and you drop it in there. Then we count and announce.

LOTS OF PROPOSALS are about land. People see an eye-sore, and they need a lawnmow-er, gloves and garbage bags.

THE EMPOWERMENT PLAN came out of SOUP. A design student for the College of Cre-ative Studies had been volun-teering at a homeless shelter and she came up with the idea of making coats. But was a woman there who said, "We don't need coats. We need jobs."

NOW THE WOMEN are making a lot of coats, creating lot of jobs and raising a lot of money.

BRINGING ART out of the rub-ble—that's a common Detroit story. It's slow change.

I GREW UP IN Sterling Heights in the suburbs. Its nickname is "Sterling Whites." Turns out Detroit is the community I've always wanted to be in.

⋙ JOHN CARLISLE ⋘

JOURNALIST

I LIKE FLYOVER country, the people no one has ever heard of.

I HAD A JOB in the suburbs for a decade. Zoning meetings, the ladies flower sale, a lot of high school sports. I was bored to death.

YOU CAN GET a front-page story on the sidewalk in Detroit.

THERE WAS this guy who fixed lawnmowers on an empty lot on Gratiot.

GUYS LIKE HIM become like a sun. He was a center of energy and the derelicts started gravitating to him.

HE GOT STABBED twice last year, and the second one killed him.

IN THE OLD auto factory days, anyone could get a house and car and place up north. I don't know what you do now.

THE MOST POPULAR story was a guy who'd lost everything — wife, job, house — and he opened a break repair shop in an abandoned garage. And at night, he'd scrawl self-help slogans all over the walls. He wanted to change his psychology, he said.

REPORTERS WITH a notepad look like the police.

IT MIGHT BE hour seven before they tell you the most important thing.

SHOW UP with a TV camera, and you can get anyone to talk.

HOW DO YOU make a life for 350,000 people who can't read?

I TRY TO BE careful. One line might hurt someone for twenty years.

IF YOU WANT to have band practice at 11 o'clock just do it.

YOU CAN DO whatever you want. But you're on your own. The defining thing about Detroit is that you are on your own.

EDWARD BOZEK

BUTCHER

DURING THE END of communism, many were emigrating. People would go to Italy or Greece, then to places like Australia and the United States.

I CAME TO AMERICA with $36 in my pocket. Detroit is just where I ended up.

I HAVE ALWAYS been a butcher. Since I was 14.

FIRST I WORKED for another grocery. They went from making just a little bucket of sausage to making hundreds of pounds.

BOZEK'S IS A place people can get things from Poland. People come from all over, Ann Arbor, Orchard Lake, Port Huron, just for the Polish newspaper.

WHEN I OPENED the butcher shop, there was big competition in Hamtramck already, two and three generations of butchers.

IF I GET MEAT today, it means the pig was walking around two days ago. I call it "smiling meat." It's the freshest.

I ONLY USE SALT, pepper and garlic — real garlic. Not the powdered.

I CURE IT, salt it, let it sit for a day, grind it, stuff it, and then I smoke it.

LIFE WAS VERY different in Poland.

I REMEMBER STANDING in line for things like coffee and sugar, bread and milk. You had to get in line at 4am.

I TOOK THE DRIVER'S test not speaking any English. Passing was like winning the lottery.

I BOUGHT A Chevy Chevette for $150 and an engine separate. I changed it out with a butter knife and one adjustable wrench.

IF WARSAW AFTER the war can be rebuilt, then Detroit can do the same.

DAVID GLENN &
MATTIE TOWNSEND

»» ««

BUS DRIVERS

DAVID: The most important thing: those mirrors. Stay on those mirrors.

MATTIE: We're completely alert at all times. Somebody might dart out, turn in front. And oh the wheelchairs.

D: They ride right down the middle of the street.

M: When you have a route that's heavy and you have no buses in front of you, it's hell.

D: This winter was the worst since the 1800's. People were waiting on a bus in the open air for over an hour. And it was like 15 degrees below zero.

M: In the winter, a lot of them break down. Summer, too.

D: Folks count on you. You're their lifeblood, basically. You have to get them where they've got to go.

M: There are a lot of streets I'd never want to go down.

D: Chalmers is one of those. It looks like Beirut. At night, people run stoplights like crazy. They don't want to stop.

D: Our favorite passenger was named Ms. T. She was like 6'6", a big woman, and you better not say nothing to her bus driver!

M: She carried a cane and she would use it.

D: It's like riding in a car with two kids in the backseat. They scream and you just keep on driving.

M: It doesn't matter what you say to the airheads and the hotheads.

D: There've been times when school kids get on and say, "My mom couldn't give me the money today." Well, my thing is, "You going to school, so have a seat."

ESSAYS

*Stories from local writers about a small slice of utopia,
the Bohemian Social Club, Lester Bangs and the
Stooges, as well as a selection of Detroit poetry*

⫸ THE VILLAGE ⫷

Written by **ROLLO ROMIG** | **IT'S NOT AS IF** we spent two decades cowering in fear. Our neighborhood was North Rosedale Park, on the northwest side, and for nearly two decades the beautiful things about living there easily eclipsed the crimes that finally drove us away. But the crimes and the beautiful things were never easy to disentangle.

We moved to North Rosedale in December, 1975, just after I turned one and my sister turned three. My mom thought she'd gone to heaven. The day we moved in our neighbor Mrs. Halsted stopped by to make sure we knew about Community Christmas — which turned out to be a beautifully organized arts-and-crafts assembly line for local kids and kaffeeklatsch for their parents, free of charge. Then our next-door neighbors the Youngs invited us to their annual Christmas party for everyone on the block. Then one night it snowed, and my parents woke up the next morning to find their sidewalk already plowed by emissaries from the neighborhood civic association. On our first Christmas at our previous house in Detroit, burglars stole our winter coats and all the presents from under the tree, leaving a stampede of muddy footprints on the living room carpet.

My parents had no idea what a paradise North Rosedale could be until they moved in. All they knew was that they could buy a gorgeous house there for only $30,000, and that was good enough. It was a big yellow-brick colonial, built solid in 1928 and clearly designed for a family with means: A wood-burning fireplace in the living room; a leaded-glass window on the stair. Down the center of the house, a two-story laundry chute. [I desperately wanted to throw my sisters down it but the doors were too small.] In the walls, a network of talking pipes — a primitive yet magically effective form of intercom. Best of all, in the basement, not one but two secret rooms. The sheer marvelousness of the place coupled with my father's modest publishing-company salary made for some ridiculous juxtapositions of luxury and frugality, like we were rebel forces who'd just captured the palace of a dictator newly fled: we'd sit in the dining room under our crystal chandelier eating store-brand cereal with powdered milk.

It was good enough that there was a lot we were willing to ignore. Five months after we moved to North Rosedale, three men with guns took my mother's purse while she chatted outside a friend's house on a perfect May evening. When a cop arrived, my dad pointed out that the muggers now had our home address and our house keys. What to do?

"Well, you go into your house, you turn off all the lights, you get your gun, and you spend the night sitting behind the front door," the cop said. "If somebody tries to come in you can start shooting."

"What is this, the fucking Wild West?" my dad said. "Anyway, I don't have a gun."

The cop rolled his eyes. What can you do with these liberals? Instead we slept at a neighbor's house — we had a hundred neighbors who would have dropped everything to host us. The next day we went back home and stayed there for another 18 years. My parents had two more daughters in that house. We never got a gun. It was the greatest place any of us have ever lived.

In moving to North Rosedale it seemed we'd unintentionally joined an intentional community. It was a neighborhood of co-ops: for nursery school, for food, for babysitting. At night a volunteer neighborhood patrol cruised the streets. When my mother was confined to bed after surgery on her spine, our neighbors got together and delivered hot dinners to our house for a month. It wasn't an ashram or a kibbutz, although there could be a slightly religious tinge to the neighborhood idealism — lots of people who lived in North Rosedale, including my parents, were committed Catholics in the social-justice vein. But if there was a single ideal that unified us, it was integration.

Detroit's record of racial segregation and housing discrimination was for much of its history so blatant and extreme that in a blind taste test you'd swear it came from the Deep South. North Rosedale had a reputation as one of the most successfully integrated neighborhoods in the city. Not that this was a competitive category - it was one of the few neighborhoods in the entire metropolitan area that was much integrated at all. The neighborhood tilted from a white to a black majority over the 18 years we lived there, but at a much slower speed than in the rest of Detroit. Black or white, the parents who moved their families to North Rosedale tended to be people who were keen on maintaining the balance. It was a modest experiment — proximity was all our parents were really asking for, especially for us kids. They simply wanted integration to seem normal to us, black and white kids together in school and on the playground, running through each other's backyards, dropping in at each other's houses for dinner.

Unlike a real intentional community, there's no interview before you arrive in North Rosedale to make sure you'll be a good ideological fit. The test was your very choice to move to the neighborhood. Detroit has been shrinking for over half a century — since well before the 1967 riots — and there are only two broad reasons why anyone stays: they have utopian ideas or they can't afford to move. Almost by definition, if you lived in North Rosedale you could have chosen to live elsewhere. It was assumed that you chose our neighborhood because you shared our collective sense of purpose. There was a certain pressure to participate. There was a real anxiety that we *needed* everyone to participate if the neighborhood was going to continue to thrive. Almost next door to North Rosedale is a neighborhood called Brightmoor, popularly known as Blight More. Much of Brightmoor matches what Detroit looks like in the popular imagination — an alarming amalgam of city dump, crime scene, and wild prairie — and it served as a warning of what could happen to us if we weren't vigilant. [Did our happy oasis in North Rosedale rely on the misery and blight that surrounded it? Sure it did. We could only afford to live there because the city as a whole was failing.] The most anxious among us formalized their commitment to the city by joining a group called The Stayers. Needless to say, not all the Stayers stayed.

What really pulled the neighborhood together was an inspired bit of urban planning. Just around the block from our house was a beautiful four-acre park, in the middle of which was the Community House, a well-used yet grand multi-purpose building owned collectively by the residents. It's difficult to overstate just how significant the Community House was. Every neighborhood should have a place like this. There was always something going on: a party, a political meeting, a play staged by the community theater company. I know that lots of neighborhoods have community centers, but this one was different. Partly it was the space itself that made it special

— the Community House was literally the center of the neighborhood, and the park set it apart like a green frame around our hive of activities. The building itself was permeated with the kinds of nooks and crannies and hiding spaces that kids live for. In the summer we transformed the Community House and grounds into a neighborhood festival called June Day, complete with a parade, a midway, and a concert in the park. In the winter we'd flood the soccer fields for ice-skating.

It was the 80s, when Detroit was best known for its murder rate and for burning itself down on Devil's Night. But if you squinted, life in North Rosedale looked almost quaint. The Fuller Brush man sold his wares door to door. The Dy-Dee truck dropped off clean cloth diapers for my baby sisters. It was like we were making a second attempt at some idealized 1950s version of American life, with parades and theater and Girl Scouts and a big neighborhood pancake breakfast on Mother's Day, only this time doing it with as much racial integration as we could muster. But the results sometimes came out twisted. I joined the neighborhood Boy Scout troop [which met at the Community House, naturally], and while we often took camping trips out in the wildernesses of Real Michigan, we didn't learn much about wildlife — our troop leaders had more enthusiasm for the flora and fauna of the city. Once were picking up trash on the median along Bretton Drive when Mr. Lawless, an ex-cop, spied a small glassine envelope. "Look, boys," he said, "you can see there are still traces of cocaine in here." Another time I asked him to identify a pair of bullet shells I'd found in my backyard. "Ah, those are .22s," he said, pleased to share his knowledge. "Probably came from a Saturday night special."

Or there was my friend Chuckie, who used to wake up early on Saturday mornings and roam the park alone looking for empty Faygo cans so he could turn them in for that sweet 10-cent Michigan deposit. The neighborhood abounded with such innocent enterprise. But one day Chuckie went home after looking through the bushes for empties and said, Dad, there's a lady sleeping in the park. And she's not wearing any clothes. Chuckie's dad went over to investigate and found a naked corpse.

> THERE WAS A REAL ANXIETY THAT WE *NEEDED* EVERYONE TO PARTICIPATE IF THE NEIGHBORHOOD WAS GOING TO CONTINUE TO THRIVE.

[*Rosedale Park*]

The restrictions our parents placed upon our freedom of movement in the park after this incident were exactly none. In the years that followed the adults related the story of Chuckie's discovery as if it were a kind of dark joke. The "lady" was "sleeping" — the things kids say! But let's put it in perspective. My uncle Tom once discovered a naked corpse in rural Ohio, in a stand of trees down by where the road curves when it reaches Lake Erie. This kind of thing could happen anywhere.

That's what we told ourselves. Or when that didn't work, we'd think of each burglary and carjacking and worse as an isolated incident, and another isolated incident, and yet another isolated incident. To live in Detroit is like having religion — it requires faith in unprovable and sometimes irrational things. To live in Detroit is to live in hope, and when people live in hope they have to ignore some things that they know are true. That's just how hope works.

But hope alone couldn't keep the chaos from seeping in. I remember wild dogs chasing me on my walk home from Cooke School; one day a whole pack of wild dogs camped out on our front porch, preventing me from going to school at all. North Rosedale was, and still is, mostly physically intact, but the preservation has come at a price. I know of one neighbor who, when the house next door to hers was abandoned, bought the house herself, renovated it from top to bottom and sold it, all to ensure that her block would remain viable. Then she did it again when another house on her block was abandoned. Then she did again for a third house.

I used to imagine that North Rosedale Park was born fully formed as an elite retreat for judges and surgeons and executives, and that Detroit's post-riot fall gave it its first taste of precarity. The actual history is entirely different. The land that's now North Rosedale wasn't developed until the 1920s; five miles of farmland separated it from Detroit proper. A photo from 1922 of my own block — on Gainsborough, the first street that was settled — shows a handful of houses on a treeless expanse in the middle of a windswept prairie. There were no schools, no stores, no garbage collection, no police. Less than a hundred years ago, the pioneers of North Rosedale were much like the residents of North Rosedale today — fretting over a dearth of city services, banding together to share resources and fight back the prairie. The neighborhood's halcyon age as a stable and secure upper-middle-class enclave lasted for maybe a single generation.

Sometimes I think of civilization itself that way - a fleeting aberration, a temporary cease-fire in a global and everlasting Wild West, a brief moment of shelter from the eternal howling prairie. Aren't we all just pioneers?

The first last straw came in 1990 — four years before we actually moved, but in retrospect it was clearly the beginning of the end. My parents spent Thanksgiving morning at Mass, then lingered for a while in the choir loft with Andy and Sally, two of our favorite neighbors from North Rosedale, while Father Serrick gave the new organ a test drive. Andy was one of the brightest presences in North Rosedale — a big friendly middle-school math teacher with a gift for fun and a tendency toward self-effacement, although secretly he was one of the engines who made the neighborhood what it was. Every encounter with Andy left you feeling better, even if you were feeling pretty good to begin with. My father was one of many people who would have liked him to be his best friend. Two days later my father went to church again, and I'll never forget the way he broke down sobbing when he came home. The only other time I'd seen him cry was after Marvin Gaye was shot to death. This time it was because he'd just found out that Andy had been murdered by burglars. At six o'clock that morning, Andy and Sally heard a loud crash from downstairs. Andy went down to investigate, and Sally heard him shout his last words: "Get out! Get out!" Then there were two gunshots and Andy bled to death on his kitchen floor.

My mother attended nearly every day of the trial. The thing that struck her most was the way one of the killers described North Rosedale Park. "It looked like a village," he said.

I had already left for college by the time my parents finally moved my younger sisters out of the city. I couldn't decide if they were smart or selling out. My younger sisters had no such ambivalence: they thought they were selling out. My parents tried to bribe them with new bicycles. We'd never been able to keep bikes in the city; even the worst 3-speed beaters would get stolen as soon as we got them home. But what's a new bike when you've had Detroit?

What North Rosedale really gave us was an occasion to rise to. The disaster of Detroit can be tremendously demoralizing - our neighbor Carol Anne had a theory that everyone who lives in Detroit is clinically depressed, and that someone ought to send crop dusters over to spray the whole city with Prozac. [In her darker moods, my mother used to say that they should empty the whole city out and nuke it.] But disaster can also deliver a jolt of purpose - something to live for beyond comfort or safety or personal amusement. Maybe people stay in Detroit because they know that the city heightens their need for their neighbors. Our vulnerability made us huddle together, and we wanted to have to huddle together. Community is a reflex that's sharpened by necessity. I have a young daughter of my own now, and the experience is oddly reminiscent of living in Detroit — it's so rich and bracing in part precisely because of the fragility and craziness of the whole thing. The very real chance that a moment's lapse or bad luck could lead to awful tragedy is a large share of what makes the love so vivid. Virtually no one who has a child wishes they hadn't. Detroit was like that, too. None of my sisters or I are tempted to move back. But we've never wished we grew up anywhere else.

Journalist **ROLLO ROMIG** grew up in Detroit and now lives in Brooklyn, New York. He's written for The New Yorker and The New York Times Magazine, and is currently writing a memoir about growing up Catholic and converting to Islam.

⫸ BOHEMIAN DREAMING ⫷

Written by **REBECCA MAZZEI** | **IN THE WORLD** that is Detroit, sometimes buildings feel less like architecture and more like people. Bricked memories like Hudson's department store or the original Cass Tech. Or old Tiger Stadium. Zoot's Coffeehouse is another. I wasn't around for Zoot's, but I've listened to tons of stories about the beat-up Victorian house in Detroit's Cass Corridor, where Joni Mitchell and Lester Bangs once walked the streets. Patti and Fred Smith, too. At Zoot's bands like Blonde Redhead, Sleater-Kinney and Silver Apples all packed out the tiny room.

The Grande Ballroom is another supreme example of Detroit building myths. An Arts and Crafts-style dance hall, circa 1928, it only ran as a rock venue for a few years in the late sixties and early seventies. Its signature evening was when MC5 played a double bill with Sun Ra. Forty years later, the Grande Ballroom sits lonesome in a commercial industrial strip not far from downtown. It looks like a weathered tombstone, one memorializing a more assertive city.

The Eastown Theater. John's Carpet House. Bookies. 404 Willis. These are just a few of the dozens of unforgettable spots that have come and gone. Defunct buildings crushed by the cold of a Michigan winter, and exposed in the summer when you really see their fractured bones, as if any one of them could crumble at one more sub-bass blasting car driving by.

I see all of these buildings as more than beaten-down relics. I see them as what they were. It's one of the reasons why I still cannot pass by the Bohemian National Home. Detroit music has deep and intimate meaning for me, and much of it is buried inside the Bohemian. It's where I learned what filling a room really means. It's where I made my best friends, and where I met the love of my life, Joel. Where I served whiskies at 400 gigs, cleaning up after most of them. It's where self-determination became something real, and where I really got to know Detroit. And the sounds still reverberate inside of me.

About nine years ago, I first set foot inside the Bohemian National Home on a late Saturday morning to do an interview for the local newspaper. The directions took me down Michigan Avenue, through Corktown, Detroit's oldest neighborhood, and a bit further into the blighted part of town that nobody calls Western Market anymore, turning past the boarded up corner shop, Meat City. This wasn't a great part of town.

I was at the Bohemian to interview an Italian brick mason and artist named Jerome Ferretti. He lived in the caretaker's apartment. When I walked in, Jerome handed me a cup of coffee and a plate of eggs, and I sat down on a crushed velvet couch. He introduced his wife Sheila, a New Orleans transplant, and Joel, a guy who'd recently moved into the building. Itching to couple us up, Jerome urged Joel to tour me through the building.

We started at the other side of the building, on Tillman Street, where the front doors looked too big to even be opened. Inside, the vestibule was empty and dusty, except for an old phone booth and a doublewide staircase that led to the second story. Upstairs and to the right was a small projection room, which, over the years, would be used as an apartment by musicians. Straight ahead through some large doors was a cavernous space with 20-foot plaster ceilings. Half of it was a ballroom with a stage and a mezzanine, and the other half was a gymnasium that had hooks planted in the floor for balance beams and pommel horses.

We walked up to the stage and through a doorway to the left, which led us to a space that would later become a musician's green room. It had gorgeous built-in bookshelves. That's where Tige, a Canadian who worked construction, lived. As ingenius as he was imaginative, Tige had found old theater props and scenery, and he'd built himself a little apartment with a turreted castle and several camping tents. The whole space felt made me feel like I'd turned the dial to an obscure AM radio station.

The Bohemian National Home was built in 1914 by Prussian immigrants to be a general social hall. In 1962, the Detroit Lithuanian Home Association purchased the building. Following their tenure, it sat vacant for several years before another owner asked Jerome to move in while he repaired it. Later, a man named Jim Kennedy — aka The President, or Skeletor or Grandpa Kennedy — lived across the

hall from Jerome and Sheila. Grandpa was an artist, a former radical book distributor and a drug dealer. His room, deemed the "library," was stacked with hundreds of books on sports medicine, politics, houseplants, you name it. Grandpa moved out when Jerome caught his girlfriend stealing a jar of change. Joel came next. In comparison to Grandpa, Joel's unassuming dreams for a concert space at the Bohemian must have seemed like a welcome transition.

This was 2005. Joel was living in Grandpa's old library, and the "Bo House," as we called it, was becoming a new version of its original social self. Chattanooga's Eugene Chadbourne was the first musician to perform once Joel took over. An improvising pianist named Thollem McDonas, who was the first to play composer Claude Debussy's piano, played later, right after lifting a keg to the Bohemian's second story. Japanese percussionist Tatsuya Nakatani, the Jimi Hendrix of the gong, performed too, and, before doing so, insisted on mopping the ballroom's well-worn floors prior to his set. When legendary musician Rhys Chatham came through, he took one whiff of the place, sat down in a club chair and said, "You can still smoke inside. Detroit is so civilized."

LIVING IN A CITY WITH LITTLE TO NO INFRASTRUCTURE IS TOUGH, SO IT ATTRACTS A MOTLEY CREW.

Anyone who knows Joel will tell you that he has a knack for pulling off feats that many suits would say require a hefty business plan and multiple investors. That lumberjack of a pianist McDonas once affectionately called Joel "the laziest overachiever" he'd ever met. And so it went for Bo House. Monthly funk shows celebrating Detroit's Northern soul heritage were deemed by *Rolling Stone* to be "one of the coolest parties in America." The Annual Festival of Jazz and Improvised Music brought in sax icon Sabir Mateen, Swiss composer and pianist Sylvie Courvoisier, and Sam Rivers, a week before he was given the key to New York City. Joel refused to keep anything more than a few bucks off the door when they performed. He even sold his car to pay the top musicians four-figure fees.

Musicians like Mission to Burma rose to the top of the "get" list and sometimes when icons with huge guarantees came through, they took one look at the building wide-eyed, and either refused to take any money from us or made plans to move to Detroit. Or both.

The Sun Ra Arkestra under the direction of Marshall Allen loved the place so much that they played an extra set to a packed house at 1 am in the morning. What I'm saying is that this is what the building pulled out of people. They felt attracted to it, compelled by it, drawn into something more than the space.

In Detroit, a music venue of this size becomes like a center for civic life. The Bo House, and others like it, felt authentic because its flaws were apparent. In comparison to the marble of the Detroit Institute of Arts, with front steps meant to lead you into a transcendent experience, the Bo House was more like a pauper's town square.

Living in a city with little to no infrastructure is tough, so it attracts a motley crew. Through our time at the Bohemian, many characters lived there, including "Don-eye", the plumber who lived in the back bar, whose delicious pot roast made up for the stash of Playboys we'd find in the bathroom or in between Grandpa Kennedy's library of books, as well as Jennie Knaggs, a Detroiter who's the Hollerin' Champion of Wise County, Virginia, and Letcher County, Kentucky, along with her alley cat Pork Chop and her boyfriend Anderson Walworth, a musician who also builds robots.

Some of my favorite performers were three times my age. I watched Dutch drummer Han Bennink perform the melody to Thelonius Monk's "Well You Needn't" with only drumsticks on a solid wood table. I woke up to the sound of Jake screaming at a stray guest he'd found sleeping under a table, a trade-off that meant he also got to party with Frank Zappa's drummer, Jimmy Carl Black.

Detroiter Faruq Z Bey [born Jesse Davis] loomed large in the Bohemian's history of performers. He was a six-foot Black Muslim poet, musician, composer and philosopher, who spoke in many tongues. Picking him up for a gig at the Bohemian was a rare gift. Faruq really blew on his saxophone, despite the fact that he was poor enough he had to ration his oxygen tank for gigs. He was a performer and composer in the seminal band Griot Galaxy, dubbed "the sci-fi band," crucial to avant-garde jazz in Detroit in the 1970s and '80s. They used to rock out on stage in metallic face paint and long dreads. As Faruq explained it once, deadpan: "Chrome on the car, chrome on your face." They were rising to international fame when Faruq was in a motorcycle accident that put him in a coma for several months. The accident effectively meant the end of the band.

In his senior years, he was hunched over but still cut an imposing figure. He lived on the east side of Detroit in a bad part of town just a few streets away from the neighboring city of Grosse Pointe, one of the state's wealthiest suburbs. He was too proud to ever let anyone inside his home. He'd take his time getting down the concrete steps and into the car. If he were in the mood, he would dive into thought and then say a few words that would stun you into silence.

The Bohemian also taught me about the inevitability of passing time. Tige, Joel, and Jerome worked on the building round the clock. Together they fixed whatever nature and time hurled at them, be it a caving roof in the dead of winter or second-story windows shattered by a light summer rain. The dream world we lived in would diminish on occasion with an outsider's admonishment. A friend of a friend would show up for a concert quite confused and quickly remind us that to "really fix this place up". . ."would cost more than a million," as if to point out that the world we were living in wouldn't really last long.

It really did feel like more than a world. The Bohemian was a galaxy, and we were all orbiting inside of it. The decrepitude and wear of the Bohemian's long years of vacancy contrasted sharply to the hours of labor we put into the place over time. So the question: Could we keep the whole thing from destroying itself?

The night before we left the Bohemian for good, I had a nightmare. In it, the building's owner was being tortured in the ballroom. I was downstairs at Jake's place, and I could hear the torture. Maybe it was the Czechs trying to take back their place, or maybe aggressor was another version of me, a darker side of myself. Whatever it all meant, it was jarring, and it told me that our time was up.

Joel and I have a new space now, a practical building that's not pretty but has great energy. It's a former spice warehouse that smells of cardamom and black pepper. Before that, the lot housed a black-owned theater called the Jewel, and before that, a Syrian boarding house. We call it Trinosophes, which roughly means three wisdoms. Here, my Detroit family has expanded. David is a Hare Krishna who works at the fish market across the street and blasts through the doors every morning, bellowing "What it iiizzzzz." And there is Earl, a frail grandfather type who stops in daily to help us clean up in exchange for some bus fare. He is a kind, honest man with fine features and a whimsical sense of humor for all the tough times he's seen.

To this day I can't drive within 30 feet of Butternut and Tillman, where the Bohemian still sits, crumbling. This is what buildings do to you in Detroit. You celebrate with them and grieve with them and dream with them.

REBECCA MAZZEI is the owner of Trinosophes in Eastern Market, a former arts critic for *Metro Times* and special projects director at the Museum of Contemporary Art Detroit.

⫸ THE STOOGES ⫷

Originally published by Stereo Review *in July* 1973

Written by **LESTER BANGS** | **THE BIGGEST TREND** on the rock circuit this year is decadence. Go to any concert, and you'll be amazed at the sudden change in American youth, who are now as far from last year's organic coveralls and bushy hanks of hair as they are from the madras shirts and slacks of 1963; teenagers of both sexes are piling on clots of make-up and swaddling themselves in flashily indeterminate glad rags. Boys with rouge and glitter on their eyelids, girls with the stark white faces and rinsed-out blonde hair of the Marilyn Monroe look they picked up from the drag queens in Andy Warhol movies — all of them seem to be a mite confused as if they'd just seen *Cabaret* and decided that whatever all *that* was, they wanted its trappings. But they're working very hard at it nonetheless, and embracing as well a whole new set of pop idols consonant with this all-out sprint toward chic degeneracy: the actually rather tame showman Alice Cooper, David Bowie, the fey mime with a brilliant publicity machine, and rafts of kohl-eyed stragglers mincing in their wake. Somehow, though, it all comes off as synthetic and as ultimately emotionless as the audience's gingerly experimentation with their own sexual identities. And every bit of it is missing that essential spark, that certain urgency that is at the root of all great rock-and-roll.

Shake hands, then, with Iggy and the Stooges, the latest and last word in shock-rock. You may find yourself repulsed by them, you may not be able to abide a single note of their music, but they are undeniably the sound and look of the future. The Stooges surpass their competition in this murky area of pop by taking all the elements that have made the Bowies and Coopers suddenly [and transitionally? Potent — glitter, sexual confusion, sub cultural shock, a sense of the garish and lurid — and adding to these a staggering dose of bone-scraping rock frenzy straight from the heart of adolescent darkness.

Another reason the Stooges loom so large among nascent glitter rockers is that, like Lou Reed [who has influenced them greatly], they were shoving this sort of thing at the world and the rock audience long before either was ready for it; they were the originators. In 1968 the Stooges were putting on shows in which lead singer Iggy Pop would fling his scabbed body to the floor of the stage in a truly convincing display of the self-destructive impulse at its purest, whereupon he would proceed to perform fellatio on the microphone while his lead guitarist jabbed him brutally from behind with the neck of his instrument. It was crude, even disgusting, but the Stooges were innovators of a sort, and both Bowie and Cooper have freely looted Iggy's stage act for gimmicks to beef up their own highly controlled but rather cold shows.

Iggy claimed that he taught everybody else in the band to play their instruments, and when their first album came out I believe they had all been playing for only about two years. It was, as was observed at the time, a *reductio ad absurdum* of rock-and-roll, but it was also music that was totally impossible to ignore and successful on its own aboriginal terms: hypnotic repetitions of a single thunderous chord at a volume that would reduce dogs to agony, over which Iggy would croon and bark and shriek improvised gut-level ditties about adolescent torments in a voice rather like some henbane mutant shade of Mick Jagger. They were songs about being lonely, shy, and awkward; they were fidgety, self-pitying rants about having *No Fun*; and, most of all, they were about sexual inadequacy and in-experience, with a strong

THE BY-NOW BANAL WORDS "HEAVY METAL" WERE INVENTED FOR THIS GROUP, BECAUSE THAT'S ALL THEY'VE GOT.

accent on the ultimate confusion of the two. Identity-crisis music on a perhaps too-basic level, it was as extreme in its aggressive neurosis as everything else about the Stooges. If ever there was a band predicated upon extremism on all levels, this was it — they ended up wasted on drugs, dropped by their record company, their instruments repossessed.

For better or worse, though, time has vindicated the Stooges, and 1973 will see them making a comeback of major proportions. They are possessed of a monomaniacal fury so genuine that it makes the posturings of Bowie and the cheery, beery Alice Cooper seem like something from a Ross Hunter production. Their new album is called *Raw Power*. And that's exactly what it delivers. *Raw Power* may be too much for many listeners to take. The by-now banal words "heavy metal" were invented for this group, because that's all they've got, and they're brutal with it: rampaging guitar lines hurtling out or or colliding like opiated dervishes, steady, mindless, four-four android drumming, Iggy outdoing even his own previous excesses with a ragged tapestry of yowls, caws, growls, raspy rants, epithets, and imprecations. The song titles tell the story: 'Search and Destroy', 'Death Trip'. The ferocious assertiveness of the lyrics is at once slightly absurd and indicative of a confused violently defensive stance that's been a rock tradition from the beginning: "I'm the runaway son of the nuclear A-Bomb/I am the world's forgotten boy...."

It's the essential terror and pain of growing up, and nowhere in rock-and-roll has it been rendered more vividly — or more energetically — than by this bunch of acne-ridden social reprobates who seem to have made a career out of *not* growing out of their teenage traumas. Whether you laugh at them or accept their chaotic rumble on its own terms, they're fascinating and authentic, the apotheosis of every parental nightmare.

LESTER BANGS was a force of nature and a legend in rock journalism. An early free-lancer for *Rolling Stone*, Bangs moved to Detroit to work at *CREEM* magazine in the mid-70s. Fearless in his opinions and radical in voice, Lester Bangs died from an accidental drug overdose in New York in 1982. His work is anthologized in two collections, *Psychotic Reactions and Carburetor Dung: The Work of a Legendary Critic* and *Main Lines, Blood Feasts, and Bad Taste: A Lester Bangs Reader*.

⫸ SELECTED POEMS ⫷

Notable works from award-winning poets
who've called Detroit home

THOSE WINTER SUNDAYS
By Robert Hayden

Sundays too my father got up early
and put his clothes on in the blueblack cold,
then with cracked hands that ached
from labor in the weekday weather made
banked fires blaze. No one ever thanked him.

I'd wake and hear the cold splintering, breaking.
When the rooms were warm, he'd call,
and slowly I would rise and dress,
fearing the chronic angers of that house,

Speaking indifferently to him,
who had driven out the cold
and polished my good shoes as well.
What did I know, what did I know
of love's austere and lonely offices?

1934

By Philip Levine

You might hear that after dark in towns
like Detroit packs of wild dogs took over
the streets. I was there. It never happened.
In the old country before the Great War,
my people were merchants and butchers,
and then the killings drove the family
first to England, then Canada, then here.
My father's brother had a shoe repair shop
for a time on Brush Street; he'd learned
the trade from his father back in Kiev.
My mother's family was in junk. The men
were huge, thick chested, with long arms
and great scarred hands. My uncle Leo
could embrace a barrel of scrap metal,
laugh out his huge laugh, and lift it up
just for the joy. His wife, Rebecca,
let her hair grow out in great wiry tangles
and carried her little fists like hammers.
Late summer Sundays we'd drive out
to the country and pick armloads
of sweet corn, boil them in sugar,
and eat and eat until we couldn't.
Can you believe those people would let
dogs take what was theirs, would cross
an ocean and a continent to let
anyone or anything dictate?
After dark these same men would drink
out on the front steps. The neighbors claimed
they howled at the moon. Another lie.
Sometimes they told stories of life

back in Russia, stories I half-believed,
of magic escapes and revenge killings,
of the gorgeous Ukrainian girls they had.
One night they tore up the lawn wrestling, until
Leo triumphed, Leo in his vested suit,
gray and sweat-stained. My uncle Josef
was different; tall and slender, he'd
come into the family through marriage
here in Michigan. A pensive, gentle man,
when stray dogs came to the back door
of the shoe shop he'd let them in, even
feed them. Their owners, he told me,
barely had enough to feed themselves.
Uncle Josef would take a battered pair
of work shoes and cut the soles off
with a hooked cobbler's knife and then,
drawing one nail at a time from his mouth,
pound on a new sole. He'd pry off
the heel and do the same. I was just a kid,
seven at most, and never tired of watching
how at the polishing wheel the leather
took on its color and began to glow.
Once he made a knife for me, complete
with a little scabbard that looped
around my belt. The black handle, too,
was leather, taken from a boot no one
reclaimed. He pounded and shaped it
until it felt like stone. Whenever you're
scared, he told me, just rub the handle
three times and nothing bad can happen.

BLACKBOTTOM
By Toi Derricotte

When relatives came from out of town,
we would drive down to Blackbottom,
drive slowly down the congested main streets
- Beubian and Hastings -
trapped in the mesh of Saturday night.
Freshly escaped, black middle class,
we snickered, and were proud;
the louder the streets, the prouder.
We laughed at the bright clothes of a prostitute,
a man sitting on a curb with a bottle in his hand.
We smelled barbecue cooking in dented washtubs,
and our mouths watered.
As much as we wanted it we couldn't take the chance.
Rhythm and blues came from the windows, the throaty voice of
a woman lost in the bass, in the drums, in the dirty down
and out, the grind.
"I love to see a funeral, then I know it ain't mine."
We rolled our windows down so that the waves rolled over us
like blood.
We hoped to pass invisibly, knowing on Monday we would
return safely to our jobs, the post office and classroom.
We wanted our sufferings to be offered up as tender meat,
and our triumphs to be belted out in raucous song.
We had lost our voice in the suburbs, in Conant Gardens,
where each brick house delineated a fence of silence;
we had lost the right to sing in the street and damn creation.
We returned to wash our hands of them,
to smell them
whose very existence
tore us down to the human.

GEORGE

By Dudley Randall

When I was a boy desiring the title of man
And toiling to earn it
In the inferno of the foundary knockout,
I watched and admired you working by my side,
As, goggled, with mask on your mouth and shoulders bright
with sweat,
You mastered the monstrous, lumpish cylinder blocks,
And when they clotted the line and plunged to the floor
With force enough to tear your foot in two,
You calmly stepped aside.
One day when the line broke down and the blocks reared up
Groaning, grinding, and mounted like an ocean wave
And then rushed thundering down like an avalanche,
And we frantically dodged, then braced our heads together
To form an arch to lift and stack them,
You gave me your highest accolade:
You said: "You not afraid of sweat. You strong as a mule."
Now, here, in the hospital,
In a ward where old men wait to die,
You sit, and watch time go by.
You cannot read the books I bring, not even
Those that are only picture books,
As you sit among the senile wrecks,
The psychopaths, the incontinent.
One day when you fell from your chair and started at the air,
With a look of fright which sight of death inspires,
I lifted you like a cylinder block, and said,
"Don't be afraid
of a little fall, for you'll be here
A long time yet, because you're strong as a mule."

THE WORKER
By Richard W. Thomas

My father lies black and hushed
Beneath white hospital sheets
He collapsed at work
His iron left him
Slow and quiet he sank

Meeting the wet concrete floor on his way
The wheels were still turning-they couldn't stop
Red and yellow lights flashing
Gloved hands twisting knobs-they couldn't stop
And as they carried him out
The whirring and buzzing and humming machines
Applauded him
Lapping up his dripping iron
They couldn't stop

JAILBREAK

By Quincy Vanderbilt

Detroit is a city
of caged brains,
of fogged eyes
that refuse to see
through a wall
where we want to go:
of singing mouths
that want to cry out
to the world about
the talents inside
our bodies,
like wild horses
trying to be broken:
of muscled arms
that want to wrap
up entire libraries,
museums & history,
like a boa constrictor
that will swallow it
into our brains.

Detroit is a city
of skilled finger
that manipulate
our imaginations
like we're puppets:
of rooted legs
that refuse to uproot
so we can climb
over hot iron walls:
of hearts that pump
oxygen to those brains
so that if they get
big enough, maybe,
just maybe, we can
bust out of that cage
& grow to become
beautiful flowers.

CITY NIGHTS
By Naomi Long Madgett

My windows and doors are barred
against the intrusion of thieves.
The neighbors' dogs howl in pain
at the screech of sirens.
There is nothing you can tell me
about the city
I do not know.

On the front porch it is cool and quiet
after the high-pitched panic passes.
The windows across the street gleam
in the dark.
There is a faint suggestion of moon shadow
above the golden street light.
The grandchildren are upstairs sleeping
and we are happy for their presence.

The conversation comes around to Grampa Henry
thrown into the Detroit River by an Indian woman
seeking to save him from the sinking ship.
[Or was he the one who was the African prince
employed to oversee the chained slave cargo,
preventing their rebellion, and for reward
set free?]
The family will never settle it; somebody lost
the history they had so carefully preserved.

Insurance rates are soaring.
It is not safe to walk the streets at night.
The news reports keep telling us the things
they need to say: The case
is hopeless.

But the front porch is cool and quiet.
The neighbors are dark and warm.
The grandchildren are upstairs dreaming
and we are happy for their presence.

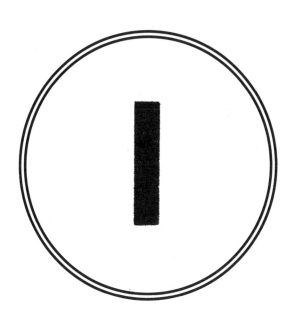

INDEX

⫸ INDEX ⫷

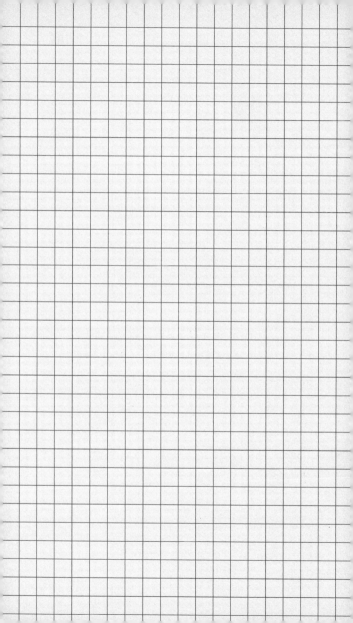

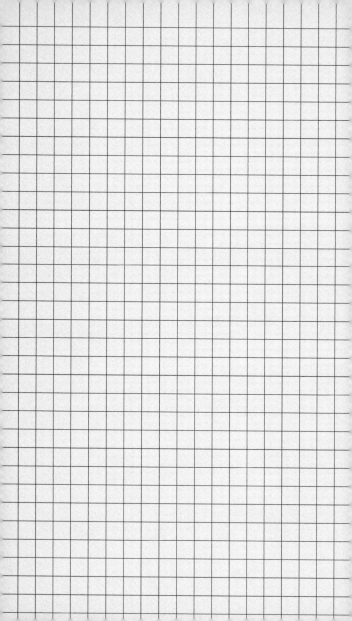

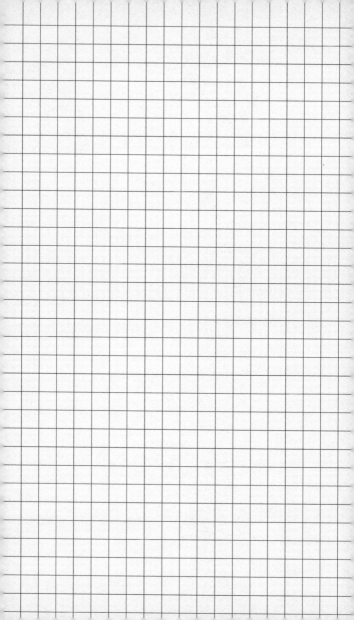

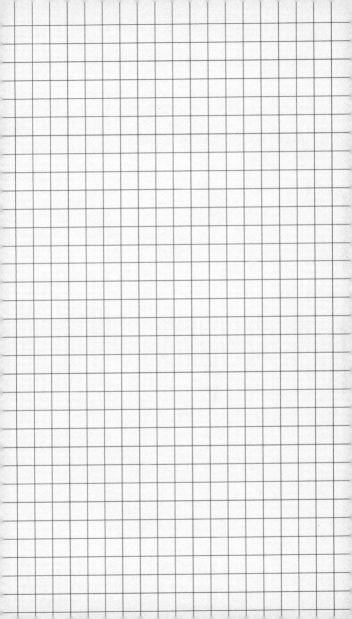

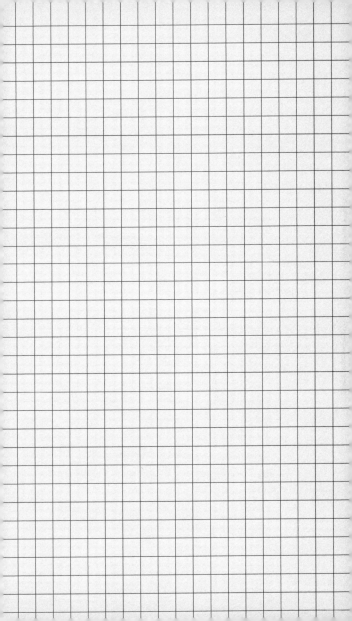

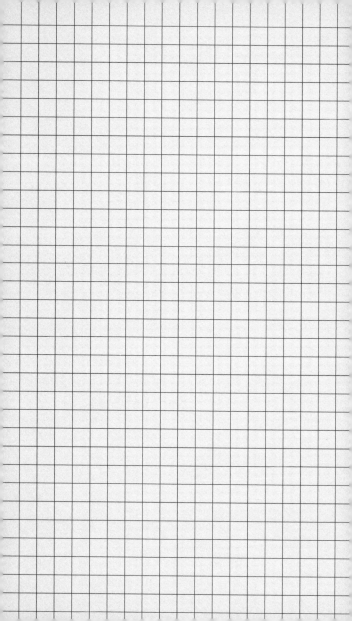

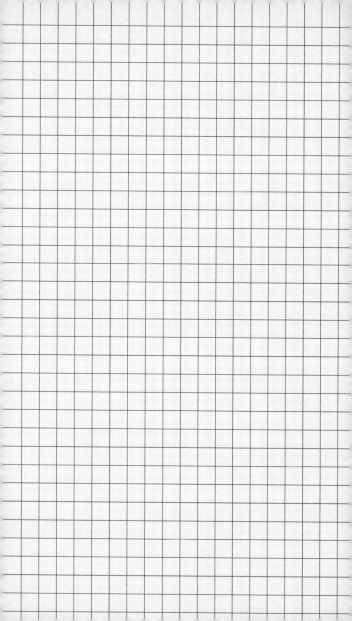

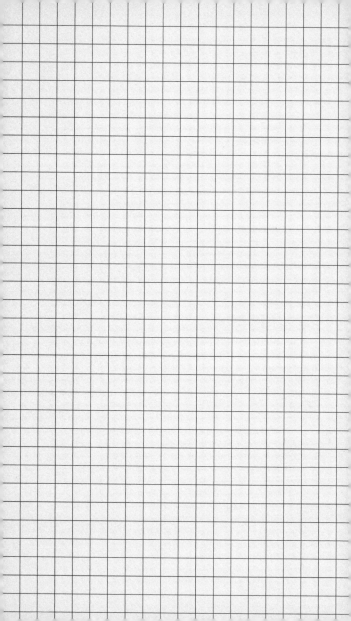

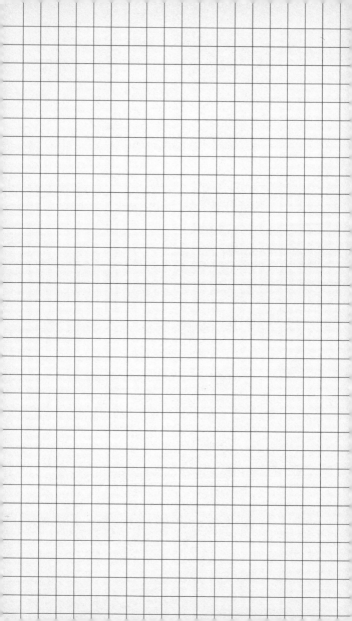